DELAWARE
PROHIBITION

DELAWARE
PROHIBITION

MICHAEL MORGAN

THE
History
PRESS

Published by The History Press
Charleston, SC
www.historypress.com

First published 2021

Manufactured in the United States

ISBN 9781540248145

Library of Congress Control Number: 2021934093

CONTENTS

CONTENTS

PREFACE

elaware Prohibition is a portrait of the First State during the battle between the wets and the drys over the manufacture and sale of illegal booze. This book paints a picture of a time that was highlighted by blazing gunfights, brazen rumrunners and illicit stills. The intent of this book was not to present an encyclopedic list of every backyard still that was discovered or every bootlegger who was arrested; the aim of this book was to present a snapshot of life in Delaware at a time when alcoholic beverages were illegal.

The passage of the Eighteenth Amendment and the Volstead Act, combined with Delaware's Loose Law and Klair Law, made the first state officially bone dry, but Delaware's appetite for alcohol was not so easily quenched. During the thirteen years that Prohibition was in effect, bootleg liquor was produced in stills that were hidden in Wilmington houses, on Kent County farms and in southern Delaware forests. Illegal hooch was brought into Delaware from Pennsylvania and across the state's long border with Maryland, the only state that did not pass legislation to support federal enforcement of Prohibition. The boundary line between Maryland and Delaware ran through rural areas, where the population was sparse and the support of bootleggers was strong. Despite optimistic proclamations that illicit booze was being driven from Delaware, bootleg liquor was available throughout Prohibition.

Delaware bootleggers and rumrunners—like all who operate outside of the law—did not keep many written records that might have been used to incriminate them; therefore, this book is drawn mainly from

A smiling "bootlegger" poses as she slips a whiskey bottle into her high boot. The swastika in the tile floor was a decorative motif that was not connected to the Nazi Party of Germany. *Courtesy of the Library of Congress.*

newspaper accounts of these nefarious activities. The online collection of the Wilmington *Sunday Morning Star* proved to be an invaluable source of information. Also, the Delaware Digital Newspaper Project, an ongoing endeavor that is regularly adding newspapers to its searchable database, was critical in preparing the early chapters of this book.

Just over a century has passed since Prohibition began, and during those one hundred years, some conventions of spelling and grammar have changed. In direct quotations, a few words that do not affect the meaning have been modernized. *Whiskey* is spelled with an "e" throughout, "state" is not capitalized and punctuation, particularly commas, have been brought up to date. Although rum is a particular type of liquor distilled from molasses, during Prohibition, "rum" was used as a generic term for any distilled alcoholic beverage.

It would not have been possible to write this book without the help of the dedicated people who staff Delaware's libraries, archives and historical societies. For their assistance, I would like to thank Michael DiPaolo, who was formerly with the Lewes Historical Society; Nancy Alexander of the Rehoboth Historical Society; Norma Jean Fowler of the Laurel Historical Society; Claudia Furnish Leister of the Milford Historical Society; Joan Lofland of the Vinyard Shipyard; Laura Scharle of the Indian River Life-Saving Statin Museum; Tim Dring of the U.S. Life-Saving Service Heritage Association; and Ashley Hall of the Delaware Public Archives.

I would also like to thank my son Tom and his wife, Karla, for their support and technical assistance. Finally, I would like to thank my wife, Madelyn, for her constant editorial advice and support. She read every word in this book numerous times and spent countless hours correcting my spelling, punctuation and grammar. Without her help and encouragement, this book would not have been possible.

DELAWARE GOES DRY

JOHN BARLEYCORN IN DELAWARE

There were three kings into the east,
Three kings both great and high;
And they ha'e sworn a solemn oath
John barely corn should die.

They took a plow and plowed him down,
Put clods upon his head;
And they ha've sworn a solemn oath
John Barleycorn was dead.

—*Robert Burns*[1]

A mythical figure of English folklore, John Barleycorn began as a metaphor for the annual barley harvest and morphed into the personification of intoxicating drinks. With the ratification of the Eighteenth Amendment to the Constitution, the "noble experiment" of prohibiting the manufacture and sale of alcoholic beverages had begun. On January 16, 1920, the Wilmington *Evening Journal* intoned, "Tonight's the end of the world for J. Barleycorn."[2] Prohibition was designed to kill off John Barleycorn, and in Delaware, he had been living a long and vigorous life.

THE DRUNKARD'S PROGRESS.

This poster, "The Drunkard's Progress," was one of several nineteenth-century posters that illustrated the evils of alcohol, beginning with a drink with a friend and ending with suicide. *Courtesy of the Library of Congress.*

When European colonists arrived in Southern Delaware, they brought with them an aversion to drinking water, which was thought to carry disease. Historian Judith Quinn, who studied the eating and drinking customs of the Delaware colonists, found that the European settlers had a number of well-ingrained drinking habits. As late as 1814, the Humane Society of Wilmington published guidelines on ways to "prevent the fatal effects of drinking cold water."[3]

Eschewing water, milk was a popular beverage in rural Delaware, where dairy cows ensured that the beverage was fresh. Without artificial refrigeration, it was too difficult to keep milk from souring to make it a popular drink in urban areas. The most popular nonalcoholic drink in colonial Delaware was tea. According to noted eighteenth-century Delaware physician Dr. James Tilton, Americans drank too much tea. He recognized that the colonists had inherited their taste for tea from their British ancestors, but it was tea (and the taxes on it) that had caused the American Revolution, and he bemoaned the fact that many Americans continued to drink tea after independence had been won. According to Dr. Tilton:

> *When we were British colonists, we were forced to be subservient to the lucrative policy of the mother country: we were taught to drink tea, coffee, rum, &c., and to indulge in variety of foreign luxuries, in subserviency to their carrying trade.... This gave occasion to our disunion; considering we had spirit and energy enough to separate from so unjust a nation of merchants.*[4]

Tilton liked to drink homegrown beverages. "Although I have quit the use of wine, along with other foreign luxuries, I indulge in a cheering glass of spirit and water, once or twice a day." He preferred "good rye whiskey or high-proof apple brandy; for I scorn to go abroad for anything that I can get better at home."[5]

Delaware colonists were also fond of a wide range of alcoholic beverages. Beer was brewed by tavern owners to serve to their customers, and many Delaware settlers brewed beer at home. Johan Risingh, the last governor of New Sweden, wrote home to obtain a wife who could tend the garden, milk the cows, spin wool into thread, tend the fishnets, cook and "brew the ale," among other duties.[6]

Risingh may have been the most prominent Delaware colonist who wanted a wife who could brew beer or ale, but he was not the only one. In the days before artificial refrigeration, nearly all beer was brewed locally, most often by settlers' wives.[7] These brewers were not always content to produce bland drinks. According to John Medkeff Jr. in *Brewing in Delaware*, "The lack of available raw materials often forced the state's 17th-century Swedish and Dutch settlers to improvise by supplementing the ales they made with native fermentables, such as persimmons, pumpkins, gourds and Indian corn. They sometimes spiced their beer with birch, sassafras, spruce, and myrtle when hops were in short supply."[8]

Wine was not uncommon on many colonial tables, and there was a winery in Southern Delaware at Lewes on Pilottown Road. Tradition has it that the winery was established by a French colonist whose vineyards produced wine for many years.

In addition to beer, hard liquor was served on many early Delaware tables. Rum was a popular ingredient in many colonial drinks. Rum was mixed with water, sugar and lemon or lime juice to produce a punch that was served cold. Warm rum mixed with sugar and allspice was usually served at funerals, and a mixture of rum, water and sugar known as "mamm" was a common tavern drink. The colonists also used rum in concoctions that were known as cherry bounces, flips, syllabubs and other lively names.[9] Grog, a mixture of rum and water, was the traditional drink of seamen, but it did little to improve their health. The poor diets on most ships made scurvy a common sailor's aliment. In 1611, Lord de la Warr sailed to Virginia with provisions for the Jamestown colony. During the voyage, Lord de la Warr contracted scurvy. After stopping at Virginia, he sailed to the West Indies, where he ate oranges and lemons and regained his health. Lord de la Warr recommended that citrus fruits become a permanent part of every sailor's diet, and eventually, British sailors were required to take a daily dose of lime juice, giving them the nickname "Limeys."

Archaeologists studying the artifacts that were recovered with the remains of the *De Braak*, which sank off Cape Henlopen in 1796, have been able to paint a detailed picture of the drinking habits sailors in the late eighteenth century. At that time, both American and British ships were well-stocked with wine, port, sherry and brandy, which were generally reserved for the captains and officers. Beer was the sailor's usual beverage, and the average seaman was issued a gallon of beer per day. The large number of glasses, tumblers, decanters and other tableware that were recovered from the *De Braak* indicate that the average sailor drank their beer from fine ceramic containers instead of the crude wooden tankards that had once been common on ships. In addition, archaeologists found a cylinder-shaped bottle marked "ketchup" among the *De Braak* artifacts. Recipes for ketchup in the late eighteenth century were much different from the tomato-based

Artifacts retrieved from the *De Braak*, which sank off Cape Henlopen in the late eighteenth century, revealed that some of the crew used silver spoons and fine ceramics. *Photograph by Michael Morgan.*

paste that is popular today. Seamen used a condiment that was a mixture of mushrooms, spices and beer.[10]

In addition to being a table beverage, rum was thought to have had a number of medicinal qualities. A mix of rum and mint was thought to improve the stomach, and a mixture of rum, milk, sugar and nutmeg was considered a cure for dysentery. Although early Delaware farmers had their backyard stills, distilled spirits did not need to be refrigerated and could be transported to customers far from the distillery. Whether it was brewed locally or distilled overseas, John Barleycorn was deeply ingrained in Delaware society in the nineteenth century, when Wilmington began to emerge as a major metropolitan area.

BEER IS LIQUID BREAD IN DELAWARE SALOONS

The secret of perfect health. Write it, talk, it sing it, shout it, 'till all human wrecks are saved.
—*advertisement for Stoeckle's beer*

As the saying goes, Delaware has three counties, two at high tide. The low, level land of the two southernmost counties, Kent and Sussex, are marked by slow-moving rivers that empty into Delaware Bay and the Atlantic Ocean, whose tidal waters often threaten to inundate the land. The shore of the bay is often marshy, and most of the river towns sit several miles from the bay. Lewes, a salty maritime town near Cape Henlopen at the

The shading shows the three counties of Delaware, from north to south, New Castle, Kent and Sussex. *Courtesy of the Delaware Public Archives.*

mouth of the Delaware Bay, had been the Sussex County seat during the colonial period—until 1791, when it was displaced by Georgetown in the center of the county. The Nanticoke River, which runs through Maryland and empties into the Chesapeake Bay, dominates the western side of Sussex County and flows near the towns of Seaford and Laurel. Astride the border with Maryland, the Great Cypress Swamp, once a fifty-thousand-acre morass of wetlands and cypress trees known as the Delaware Everglades, hid vagabonds, highwaymen and, at times, moonshiners.

Although small crossroad towns dotted the Delaware landscape, most people lived on farms where some of the houses were astonishingly small. Some contained less than four hundred square feet, smaller than modern garages.[11] Often, a collection of pens, barns and other crude farm buildings where farmers kept their livestock, brewed their beer and distilled their whiskey surrounded the houses.

North of Sussex County lay Kent County, with more small farms, fewer rivers and Dover, the state capital. Geographically positioned in the middle of the state, Dover, the county seat of Kent County, was a small, normally quiet town—except when it was swollen by the lawmakers, lawyers and lobbyists when the legislature was in session. With no port or deepwater facilities and little industry, Dover had little potential to become a big city. That claim would go to Wilmington.

In the northern reaches of New Castle County, Wilmington was separated from the rest of the state by the new Chesapeake and Delaware Canal that cut across New Castle County fifteen miles south of the city. In the nineteenth century, Wilmington emerged from the shadow of Philadelphia thirty miles to the north. Containing some of the highest ground in the state, topping off at nearly 450 feet, Wilmington is nestled between Brandywine Creek and the Christina River, near where the two waterways merged and flowed into the Delaware River. The Christina River was blessed with port facilities capable of accommodating oceangoing vessels. The swift-moving Brandywine Creek provided power for grist, textile and paper mills, but most importantly, it provided power for the Du Pont powder mills.

Eleuthere Irenee du Pont de Nemours, a pupil of noted French chemist Antoine Lavoisier, founded a high-quality gunpowder mill on Brandywine Creek in 1802.[12] The du Pont mills quickly developed into the premier gunpowder factory in the United States and made the du Ponts one of the wealthiest families in America, a distinction that continues to this day.

Owned by the Penn family as a colony, Delaware had long been the stepchild of other governments. First settled by the Dutch and Swedes,

Taken a decade before Prohibition, this photograph shows the growing Wilmington area. *Courtesy of the Delaware Public Archives.*

Delaware was harassed by Maryland until the colony had been taken over by the English and acquired by William Penn, who wanted it to protect the maritime approaches to Pennsylvania. Known as the "Three Counties on the Delaware," the colony was the least of Penn's holdings, and the American Revolution had given Delaware independence from Pennsylvania as well as from Great Britain. When the Constitution was written, Delaware, the least populous state, saw it as an opportunity to protect itself from the domination of the larger states. Delaware was the first to ratify the Constitution and bore the nickname "First State" proudly. A slave state since its founding, Delaware's deep devotion to the Union remained during the Civil War.

In the nineteenth century, some Delaware towns were large enough to support taverns that brewed their own beer, but the growth of Wilmington far outpaced the rest. At the dawn of the twentieth century, Wilmington, with over seventy-six thousand residents, had 40 percent of the First State's population that supported dozens of taverns and hotels. On the eve of Prohibition, the *Wilmington Sunday Morning Star* commented:

> *An interesting feature of saloons in Delaware is the fact that all licenses were granted as inn and tavern licenses and were granted to permit not only sale of intoxicating liquor but conduct of a hotel with all accompaniments,*

such as stable, boardinghouse and the like. In short, all facilities of the old-time inn, according to the old English type. In recent years, of course, this had been changed, and there have been no stables attached to the hostelries. The requirement that there should be rooms attached, however, still holds in case of inn and tavern licenses, although most of the other requirements have been waived.[13]

In some areas of downtown Wilmington, taverns were more prevalent than today's Starbucks, particularly in the Market Street neighborhood near the old town hall. Some of these Wilmington watering holes, such as the Indian Queen Hotel and the Delaware House, served Delaware drinkers for generations. According to the *Sunday Morning Star*:

It is alleged that in the case of one old saloon in Wilmington, still standing and until recently doing business, there was formerly a slave mart attached, where slaves were brought in the old days and sold. Various rumors are abroad of the doings of that time and one especially interesting to the effect that it was the custom for certain parties to go down the State or over into Maryland, steal slaves and dispose of them at this mart.[14]

Another view that shows Wilmington was developing into a major city. *Courtesy of the Delaware Public Archives.*

Well-known social photographer Louis Hine took a number of pictures documenting life in Wilmington before Prohibition. *Courtesy of the Library of Congress.*

Outside of Wilmington, there was also a scattering of saloons in Dover, Georgetown and Lewes.

After the Civil War, the advent of artificial refrigeration and pasteurization enabled brewers to dispatch their products to distant destinations, and this drove most of the local breweries out of business. According to John Medkeff Jr.'s *Brewing in Delaware*, "The Hartmann & Fehrenbach, Stoeckle,

Above: The Hartmann and Fehrenbach Brewery closed during Prohibition. *Courtesy of the Delaware Public Archives.*

Left: A Hartmann and Fehrenbach advertisement touted that their beer was called "Liquid Bread." Sunday Morning Star, *June 9, 1907.*

and Bavarian Breweries dominated the Delaware industry from 1881 until 1919. Several other smaller firms operated as well during this period, both in and outside of Wilmington, though none could compete for long."[15]

Wilmington's "Big Three" breweries promoted their products by freewheeling and releasing unsubstantiated advertising that was common in the early twentieth century. Delaware newspapers carried advertisements for Brown's Iron Bitters that said it supposedly cured constipation, malaria, kidney and liver troubles, bad blood and "women's complaints."[16] Botanic Blood Balm, which was sold at Miller's Drug Company in Wilmington, claimed it "cures cancers of all kinds" and "many apparently hopeless cases of cancer."[17] Stoeckle advertised that its beer was endorsed by "all the most reputable physicians" and that it was "unrivaled for purity and flavor and possessing more rare and medicinal qualities than any other brand of beers brewed in America." Stoeckle's was "the secret of perfect health. Write it, talk it, sing it, shout it, till all human wrecks are saved."[18] Not to be outdone, Hartmann and

In this Hine photograph of a Wilmington newsboy, it was noted that he visited saloons. *Courtesy of the Library of Congress.*

Fehrenbach invoked the traditional bromide about the nutritional benefits of beer and declared, "Our beer is called 'Liquid Bread.'"[19]

The largest distiller in the First State was Levy's in Dover, which did little to no newspaper advertising, but Delaware newspapers frequently carried advertisements by out-of-state distillers that touted their health benefits. The

November 19, 1909 edition of the Wilmington *Evening Journal* carried an advertisement for Duffy's Pure Malt Liquor that claimed:

> *If you wish to keep young, strong and vigorous and have your cheeks the roses of heal and retain full possession of your mental powers, you must take Duffy's Pure Malt Whiskey regularly, as directed. It nourishes the vitality, no matter how week or feeble it may have become; feeds and enriches the blood and stimulates the circulation, giving health and power to body, brain, nerve and muscle. It is invaluable for overworked men, delicate women and sickly children.*[20]

CLARENCE TRUE WILSON FIGHTS ALCOHOL

The saloon must go!
—the motto of the Anti-Saloon League

With breweries, distilleries and others touting the advantages of consuming alcohol, and with few restraints on the amount of intoxicating beverages a person could drink, the average American consumed seven gallons of alcohol each year. Drunkenness was understandably common. In the nineteenth century, broken families, crime and a host of other social ills were said to be the results of overindulging in alcohol. These conditions sparked a drive to ban alcohol altogether. On May 17, 1848, William Morgan, a Sussex County native, wrote in his diary, "Today, we had a good parade of the Sons of Temperance at Laurel; the stand, 35 by 10 feet, was fixed up opposite the Presbyterian Meeting House. It was beautiful, decorated with wreaths of blue and white muslin mixed with wreaths of evergreens and roses emblematical of the Order of the Sons of Temperance."[21]

On September 29, 1842, the Order of the Sons of Temperance was formed by a few workers in New York City. The organization resolved to shield its members, known as "brothers," from the evils of intemperance, to afford mutual assistance in times of sickness and to provide thirty dolloars for burial costs at the death of a fellow brother. In the beginning, no women were allowed to be members, and a candidate for membership had to be nominated by a brother in good standing. Members of the Sons of Temperance took a solemn pledge: "*I will neither make, buy, sell nor use as a beverage, any spirituous or malt liquors, wine or cider.*" After the initial meeting,

SONS OF TEMPERANCE.

In this Sons of Temperance engraving, the man on the left holds a scroll that reads, "PLEDGE No brother shall make, buy, sell or use, as a beverage any Spiritous or Malt Liquors, Wine, or Cider." *Courtesy of the Library of Congress.*

which was held in Teetotalers Hall in 1842, chapters (known as "divisions") were soon organized in many areas along the Eastern Seaboard, including in Southern Delaware.[22]

In keeping with the overt religious nature of the organization, a Bible was presented by the ladies of Laurel to the Howard Division of the Sons of Temperance. After several ministers addressed the crowd, William Morgan recorded in his journal, "Then Lawyer Rider from Salisbury gave another address to great satisfaction. After the sons partook of an excellent dinner spread under the trees near the PMH [Presbyterian Meeting Hall] all passed excellently with plenty of cold water, a sober time!"[23]

After dinner, there were several additional speakers. According to Morgan:

> *Rev. W.C. Pool delivered an address to 400 or 500 listening spectators in which he describes the ancient Order of Drunkers. It exceeded anything we had ever heard. Some looked ashamed, some looked pale, all alighted and the sons lift up their heads. Next, the Rev. J. Varden (president of the Maryland Conference) arose and gave the closing address. He certainly is one of the* [complete] *mimics of drunkards I ever saw or heard, if not one of the greatest graphic* [speakers]. *The people never heard the like before. We marched into Laurel and disbanded. All in good order.*[24]

Following the Civil War, the work of the Sons of Temperance was overshadowed by the Woman's Christian Temperance Union (WCTU), whose most prominent member was the hatchet-welding Carrie Nation.[25] Formed in 1874, the WCTU promoted total abstinence from alcohol, tobacco and all harmful drugs. The movement to ban alcoholic beverages was strong in Southern Delaware, where Clarence True Wilson emerged as a leader in the anti-alcohol crusade.

Born in Milton in 1872, Clarence's father, John Alfred Wilson, was a Methodist minister, and young Clarence inherited a respect for religion and a hatred for alcohol. Clarence was seventeen years old when the Milton chapter of the WCTU was founded, with its first meeting being held on July 4 aboard the schooner *James M. Carey*. The next year, he became a church deacon, and two years after that, he became an elder in the Methodist Episcopal Church, and his crusade against the evils of alcohol was well underway.

Clarence True Wilson began his ministry in Seaford before he moved out of Delaware to continue his education and temperance activities. In 1906, Wilson was elected president of the Oregon Anti-Saloon League. Founded

Clarence True Wilson was a lifelong crusader against alcoholic beverages. *Courtesy of the Library of Congress.*

in 1893, the Anti-Saloon League worked to unify the growing public temperance sentiment and targeted places that sold alcoholic beverages with the motto, "The saloon must go!"[26] He helped organize the advocates of Prohibition into an effective political force through his writings. In 1912, Wilson wrote *Dry or Die: The Anglo-Saxon Dilemma*, and beginning in 1915, he was the editor of the *Pocket Cyclopedia of Temperance*. His fiery speeches and organizational efforts helped turn believers of Prohibition into an effective political force. Wilson's white hair, ruddy face, Colonel Sanders–style goatee and fiery tongue awed many who dared to oppose him. In addition, Wilson gave numerous speeches in which he harangued the evils of alcohol and the "rum element" that he believed controlled the government. Beginning in 1915, he was the editor of the *Pocket Cyclopedia of Temperance*, in which he attacked whiskey advertisements that made dubious claims, including that whiskey was "invaluable for overworked men, nervous 'rundown' women, and delicate, underdeveloped children.'"[27]

This Hine photograph shows boys at a sidewalk bar, drinking an unidentified beverage. *Courtesy of the Library of Congress.*

During the closing years of the nineteenth century, the drive to pass laws outlawing intoxicating drinks picked up steam, and shortly after the dawn of the twentieth century, the temperance movement became caught up in a series of reforms spawned by the industrialization of the United States.

THE SLOW DEATH OF JOHN BARLEYCORN

After one year from the ratification of this article, the manufacture, sale, or transportation of intoxicating liquors within, the importation thereof into, or the exportation thereof from the United States and all territory subject to the jurisdiction thereof for beverage purposes is hereby prohibited.
—Eighteenth Amendment to the Constitution

Broken families, disease, crime and other problems attributed to John Barleycorn could just as easily have been assigned to John D. Rockefeller, Andrew Carnegie, J.P. Morgan and others who aided and abetted the rapid growth of American industry in the last decades of the nineteenth century and the early years of the twentieth century. The phenomenal expansion of industry in the United States created a millionaire class whose lavish lifestyles stood in sharp contrast to the millions who lived the slums of the cities, particularly in the Northeast United States. The injustice of a government that rewarded such a disparity of wealth sparked a demand for a variety of amendments to the Constitution. In 1913, the states ratified the Sixteenth Amendment, the first change in the Constitution in over four decades that allowed the government of the United States to levy an income tax on its citizens . Not only did the income tax attempt to attack the disparity of wealth, but it also paved the way for the national prohibition of alcohol. Before the income tax, approximately 40 percent of the United States government's income came from taxes on alcohol. With the passage of the Sixteenth Amendment, the financial argument that the government needed the income from taxes on alcohol was no longer valid, and the anti-prohibitionists had lost one of their major arguments.[28]

The second reform amendment dealt with the election of United States senators, which, in Delaware, was personified by the dubious political career of J. Edward Addicks. Armed with little political experience but with a ton of money, Addicks attempted to buy one of Delaware's United States Senate seats

Born in 1841 in Philadelphia, Addicks thrived in the rough-and-tumble world of nineteenth-century capitalism. The *New York Times* said of the millionaire, "Suave, impudent, industrious and an absolute heretic regarding hereditary honesty in other men, he somehow managed, by reason of these faculties or in spite of them, to amass a fortune."[29] Having succeeded in business, he moved to Delaware, and according to the *New York Times*, "He introduced himself to Delaware politics first in a high silk hat and fur overcoat, both them curiosities, and announced to a small group of newspapermen in the state house that he was a candidate for United States senator."[30] His only political asset was a thick bank account, and for a decade and a half, Addicks lubricated the political process with every penny at his disposal.[31]

In the late nineteenth century, United States senators from Delaware and many other states were elected by the state legislatures. In 1894, many of Addicks's supporters won their elections to the Delaware General Assembly, and the Lewes newspaper, the *Delaware Pilot*, quoted other First State newspapers as saying, "When we turn to the *State Sentinel* and hear the slogan 'hold on, boys, boys, victory is in sight;' we rise as on eagles wings. But alas, how vain are all things here below, for the *News and Advertiser*, clips our wings by telling us 'that his election—Mr. Addicks—would not only mean political damnation, but a moral turpitude much more serious.'"[32] The *New York Times* characterized him as a "a truculent ruffian of the type of the Mississippi gambler who got his living by 'sitting behind four kings and a bowie knife.'"[33]

The millionaire Addicks so divided the Republican Party that it led to a deadlock in the state legislature, where no Senate candidate was able to cobble together a majority from the two Republican factions or the Democratic legislators. Durring Addicks's bid for the United States Senate, the *New York Times* editorialized, "Our esteemed contemporaries do not appear to be clear in their own minds whether Addicks wants to go to the Senate because he has too much money or because he has not enough; whether he looks at the senatorship as a pleasure for which he is willing to pay or as a business in which he desires to invest."[34]

For several years, one of Delaware's two Senate seats remained vacant, and between 1901 and 1903, the state had no U.S. Senators. The *New York Times* commented, "Strictly speaking, of course, the election of an unscrupulous 'hustler' like Addicks would be a disgrace to the state of Delaware."[35]

Addicks failed in his attempt to buy his way into the Senate, and he had passed from the Delaware political scene when the Seventeenth Amendment, which called for the election of senators by the people instead of the state legislatures, was proposed. Passed by Congress in May 1912, this amendment was ratified with lighting speed on April 8, 1913.[36]

With these two reforms out of the way, the calls for a prohibition amendment heated up. Delaware was way ahead of the game. Delaware allowed a local option to ban alcohol. The Methodist Church was in the forefront of the crusade against alcohol, and in 1908, the *Official Journal of the Forty-Fifth Session Delaware Conference Methodist Episcopal Church* confidently reported, "The Temperance people of the state of Delaware have fought long and persistently in order that the state might be rid of rum rule....The tidal wave of local option that is sweeping the country, at the special election held in November last, landed Kent and Sussex counties safely in the 'dry column' with indisputable majorities."[37]

With the banning of alcohol in Kent and Sussex Counties, two of the three counties in Delaware were dry. New Castle County, which included the city of Wilmington (which had nearly half of the state's population and most of Delaware's saloons), remained wet. This, however, did not put an end to

In this photograph, Hine captured an image of a bar (*left*) nestled between rowhouses in a Wilmington residential neighborhood. *Courtesy of the Library of Congress.*

booze in Southern Delaware. Illegal stills were set up in the Great Cypress Swamp and other dark corners of Southern Delaware, and the moonshine was carted along backcountry roads to speakeasies across Sussex County. The *Bethany Beach Booster*, a short four-page newsletter that reported news and notes about the goings on at Delaware's newest ocean resort, reported in September 1912, "WCTU [Woman's Christian Temperance Union] should be alert for traveling speakeasies in Baltimore hundred. Last Sunday afternoon, at least fifty persons at Bethany Beach witnessed a genuine display of the real stuff dumped into Mrs. Warren's yard by a runaway team that had been left in the street without a driver."[38] The small crowd that assembled after the accident presumably sampled the "real stuff" that was dumped into Mrs. Warren's yard.[39]

The transportation of liquor into the state was no laughing matter. In 1917, Representative Daniel Loose of Kent County championed a law that would make it illegal to transport alcohol into Delaware. The "Loose Law," as it was known, also banned the possession of more than a quart of liquor or a dozen pint bottles of beer.[40] The situation between the wet and dry

As this Hine image shows, horses and wagons were still common in Wilmington in the decade before Prohibition began. *Courtesy of the Library of Congress.*

areas of Delaware was intensified in November 1917, when a referendum in New Castle County on the prohibition of alcoholic beverages was held. Wilmington rolled up a wet majority by 2,259 votes, but the *Newark Post* reported, "In rural New Castle County, however, it was practically a landslide for the 'drys,' as they won every hundred in the county with the exception of [the town of] New Castle."[41] Although the production and sale of liquor in Wilmington remained legal, the *Evening Journal* pointed out, "Yesterday's vote in the rural county, coupled with the Loose Liquor anti-shipping law, will make it unlawful for liquor to be shipped from Wilmington into any part of the rural county."[42] The newspaper went on to comment on the Loose Law, "If a person carries more than one quart of liquor or more than eight bottles of beer…in an automobile from the city into the rural county, the auto could be confiscated."[43]

As the anti-alcohol forces were tightening their grip on Delaware, the United States' entry into World War I created anti-German hysteria that spilled into the prohibition movement. The war began in Europe in 1914, and by January 1916, the conflict had men mired in bloody trenches for

The German Hall indicated the strong German presence in Wilmington. *Courtesy of the Library of Congress.*

over a year. But the United States, with millions of German, Italian and other immigrants from the warring nations, was stridently neutral and remained out of the fray. The reports of aircraft bombing European cities and Zeppelins targeting London kept the eyes of some Delaware residents fixed on the skies, and they were not to be disappointed. In Wilmington, keen-eyed citizens reported seeing warplanes hovering over the Du Pont powder mills; at Dover, people spotted unidentified aircraft in the evening sky; and along the Delaware River, some saw a squadron of planes that flew from New Jersey into Delaware.

It soon became apparent that the Germans were not conducting flights over Delaware. Eventually, the authorities concluded that the supposed lights of German aircraft were, in reality, an optical illusion caused by the close conjunction of Venus and Jupiter in the early night sky. The proximity of the two planets created an unusually bright celestial display that some nervous and untrained observers mistook for the light of an aircraft.[44] The reports of German aircraft over Delaware quickly subsided, but the xenophobic frenzy against Germans, often associated with beer drinking, continued.

On December 18, 1917, nine months after the United States entered World War I, Congress passed the Eighteenth Amendment, which read, in part, "After one year from the ratification of this article, the manufacture, sale, or transportation of intoxicating liquors within, the importation thereof into, or the exportation thereof from the United States and all territory subject to the jurisdiction thereof for beverage purposes is hereby prohibited." The nearly century-old legal battle against John Barleycorn had been won.[45]

2

DOCTORS, RUMRUNNERS AND THE KLAN

No Booze for Flu

If you have no confidence in your doctors, you might as well take away his license.
—*Dr. Albert Robin, president of the New Castle County Medical Society*

"Is whiskey a drug?" On April 17, 1920, legislators, doctors and others crowded into the statehouse on the Green in Dover to hear a debate that would determine the extent of Prohibition in Delaware. After the Eighteenth Amendment was ratified, Congress passed the Volstead Act, which defined intoxicating beverages as any that contained 0.5 percent alcohol, outlawed the manufacture and sale of intoxicating beverages and provided penalties for violations of the law. The Volstead Act allowed for the manufacture of alcohol for industrial, scientific and religious purposes.[46] The law did not explicitly prohibit the dispensation of alcohol for medicinal purposes, but Delaware enacted the Klair Law (named for Aaron F. Klair of Mill Creek Hundred), which made the possession of liquor, beer and wine illegal and outlawed medicinal alcohol.[47] Some doctors were outraged, claiming that liquor was a valuable drug and that if they could not prescribe alcohol, it would cost lives.

While the states were in the process of ratifying the Eighteenth Amendment, the 1918 influenza pandemic, known as "la grippa," the "Spanish flu," or simply the "flu," spread rapidly around the world. Scientists and historians debate where the pandemic originated, but it is believed that the spread of the flu was aided by the massive shifts of military personnel toward the end of World War I. In the spring of 1918, American soldiers contracted the flu, and during the summer, the disease infected people across the United States. In the fall, it reached Newark, Delaware. By September 24, there were at least 50 cases in the Newark area and five deaths. Schools and movie theaters were closed, and the Newark Board of Health recommended, "Citizens are urged to avoid crowds or even small gatherings, to abstain from traveling on the railroads, to keep children off of the streets and to use extra precaution as to cleanliness and general hygiene."[48] At first, it appeared that the disease was held in check. On September 25, the *Wilmington Evening Journal* reported, "Although several additional mild cases of Spanish influenza have been reported in Newark and vicinity, local physicians are doing everything possible to check the spread of the disease."[49] By the end of September, however, doctors had reported 2,442 flu cases in Wilmington.[50] By December, the flu had spread across the entire state. According to the Centers for Disease Control, "The 1918 influenza pandemic was the most severe pandemic in recent history....It is estimated that about 500 million people or one-third of the world's population became infected with this virus. The number of deaths was estimated to be at least 50 million worldwide, with about 675,000 occurring in the United States."[51]

During the influenza pandemic, many doctors prescribed liquor for their patients. The use of alcohol as a drug was a deeply ingrained practice dating back centuries. In a study of 1,000 prescriptions for liquor, alcohol was prescribed for nearly fifty ailments, including abscesses, boils, chills, diabetes, insomnia, loss of appetite, nervousness and ulcerated teeth. La grippe (flu) was the second-most prescribed ailment, at 163 out of 1,000, falling just behind "general debility" at 167.[52] The Klair Law prohibited any of these uses, but in 1920, a proposed change (known as the Mcnabb Amendment) to the Klair Law was proposed to allow Delaware doctors to prescribe liquor. On April 17, 1920, the Delaware House of Representatives held a spirited hearing on the Mcnabb Amendment.

Dr. Henry W. Briggs, a prominent Wilmington physician, a member of the board of health, the director of public safety and a member of the staff of the Delaware Hospital, claimed that all the Mcnabb Amendment did was give physicians the right to prescribe alcohol and its derivatives for medicinal purposes.[53] Briggs maintained, "We are not here to argue Prohibition. We have voted for the closing of the corner saloon and stopping of the legalized liquor traffic for beverage purposes, but we did not vote or did not think we did to take away our right to prescribe liquor."[34] Briggs asserted that W. Truxton Boyce, the federal Prohibition director for Delaware, favored the amendment, and the doctor presented a petition that was signed by 125 Delaware physicians who supported the Mcnabb Amendment. Briggs closed by saying, "I am not going to argue as to the benefits of liquor as a medicine, the petition speaks for that, but we do argue for our constitutional rights."[55]

Dr. Albert Robin, president of the New Castle County Medical Society, followed Briggs and repeated the claim that they were not there to argue Prohibition. Robin said, "Most of us voted for Prohibition for the same reason that most of you did, to close out the corner saloon....That question is settled." Robin claimed that he prescribed very little liquor and said, "If you have no confidence in your doctors, you might as well take away his license."[56]

Dr. Howard A. Kelly, an eminent surgeon at the Johns Hopkins Hospital in Baltimore, opened the debate for those who opposed giving doctors the right to prescribe alcohol, which some thought might create a large loophole in the Prohibition laws. Kelly denied that alcohol was essential and questioned whether any reputable doctor had written a prescription for alcohol to treat typhoid fever or pneumonia in the past five years. The question brought jeers from the doctors in the gallery. When the hubbub subsided, Kelly went on to insist that the highest medical authorities discredited the use of alcohol, saying that he could not dignify the liquor by calling it a drug. He went on to ask, rhetorically, that if alcohol helped treat pneumonia or the flu, why were so many German beer drinkers dying like flies? When Kelly claimed that patients often died when alcohol was used to treat snake bites, the gallery erupted in laughter.[57]

Kelly was followed by Dr. L.S. Conwell, the secretary of the State Board of Health; Reverend C.L. Hubbard of Wilmington; and George W. Crabbe of Baltimore, the superintendent of the Anti-Saloon League for Maryland [and] Delaware, who all argued that the Mcnabb Amendment would weaken the enforcement of the Prohibition laws. Crabbe spoke of the danger of unscrupulous physicians abusing the Mcnabb Amendment, and he concluded, "Let it stand, and give it a year, at least, to see what it will do."[58]

In rebuttal, Dr. Robin, who led the advocates of the amendment, read a letter from Dr. Hobart Hare, a prominent Philadelphia doctor and a member of the faculty of the Jefferson Medical College. Hare considered alcohol one of the most valuable drugs available at the time, and in his own practice, he often prescribed whiskey or brandy for a variety of ailments. Briggs surprised those who opposed the amendment by reading an article by Kelly in which the Johns Hopkins surgeon had prescribed whiskey for the treatment of various conditions. The Baltimore surgeon admitted that he had written the article. Briggs also complained that the hearing had developed into a prohibition meeting and that its scientific considerations were being set aside by the hysteria of fanaticism. Under intense questioning by Briggs, Kelly agreed a physician should have the right to prescribe any drug he saw fit to use.[59]

Dr. Henry A. Cleaver praised the surgical ability of Kelly; but he said, "I protest the right of any men or set of men, clergymen or prohibitionists, to dictate to these men who have the responsibility of the life of the patient what they shall not use." Cleaver continued, "I want it understood that I am bitterly opposed to liquor as a beverage. I do not use it and think that the prohibition [of it] is the salvation of the human race."[60]

The doctors who favored the Mcnabb Amendment essentially argued that Delaware doctors had a right to prescribe whiskey in some cases and that the failure to do so was tantamount to a dereliction of duty.[61] After three hours, the debate concluded. In the end, the Mcnabb Amendment was rejected.[62] There would be no booze for the treatment of the flu or any other disease. During Prohibition, the First State was under one of the most severe restrictions of alcohol in the nation.

BONE DRY BY 1921

When the jury returned, both bottles bore evidence
of having been thoroughly tested.
—Evening Journal

"The federal prohibition amendment, which became effective Friday night," the *Wilmington Sunday Morning Star* reported on January 18, 1920, "did not create a ripple in Wilmington."[63] The effective date of the passage of the Eighteenth Amendment was preceded by Delaware's local option, wartime prohibition on the use of grain to produce alcohol, the Loose Law and the Klair Law, which effectively made the state dry. Over a week before the official start of national Prohibition, Sergeant Detective Francis Green of the Wilmington Police noticed that local resident William Fisher was transferring several wooden cases from two cars to a house on Orange Street. When Detective Green questioned Fisher, he refused to say what he was carrying into the cellar. Green went into the cellar and found thirty cases of whiskey containing 358 full fifths of booze. Fisher was arrested, but he refused to say where he got the whiskey. The next day, the police raided the home of Elmer Fisher, William's brother, on Monroe Street, where they found over seven full cases of whiskey and nearly two cases of brandy. Elmer Fisher said he had purchased the liquor before July 1, 1919, when the laws restricting the ownership of alcoholic beverages went into effect. Possession of alcohol was allowed under the Volstead Act, but under the Loose Law, it was illegal to possess more than one quart of liquor. Elmer claimed he bought it for his own use and with his own money. The Fishers were moving the liquor from Monroe Street to his father's house on Orange Street. Elmer said he wanted the alcohol so that he and his wife could rub their baby with it. Finally, he maintained that he had not taken a drink for twelve years. He, however, said he wanted to be prepared in case he started drinking again.[64]

When Elmer Fisher was tried in October 1920, the case had gained such notoriety that the *Evening Journal* reported, "The case aroused so much commotion in the public building that all business was suspended during the hearing."[65] The eighty-five quarts of liquor were brought into the courtroom as evidence, and after the case was argued, the jury retired to consider the verdict. They took with them one of the bottles of evidence to make sure that it was whiskey. After some time, the jury had not reached a decision, and the tension began to mount in the courtroom. Finally, the bailiff appeared and whispered something to the prosecuting attorney, who announced, "The jury wants another quart of whiskey." The additional evidence was dispatched to the jury room. A short time later, the jury announced that it had reached a verdict, and in the words of the *Evening Journal*, "When the jury returned, both bottles bore evidence of having been thoroughly tested." Apparently, the content of the two bottles was not strong enough for the jury's tastes, and Fisher was found not guilty and released.[66]

The arrests for bootleg liquor continued, and in May 1920, W. Truxton Boyce, the federal Prohibition officer for Delaware, announced that no booze was being sold in Wilmington to any extent.[67] In July, he reported that approximately one thousand gallons of liquor, mostly whiskey, worth $25,000, had been seized in the past year in Delaware. Boyce said that between ten and twenty arrests had been made on various bootlegging charges. Some of the vehicles that had been seized while carrying illegal liquor had been permanently confiscated. Commenting on the results of the first year of his work, Mr. Boyce said, "We believe the situation in Delaware will compare favorably with the best anywhere in the country under the eighteenth constitutional amendment. Both the amendment

A government chemist tests drinks for the strength of alcohol and impurities. *Courtesy of the Library of Congress.*

and the enforcement acts generally are respected, and there have been relatively few deliberate violators."[68]

Although Boyce believed he was clamping down on bootleg whiskey in Wilmington, in Sussex County, fifty pints of "hooch" had disappeared from the cellar of Deputy Attorney General Howard Cooks in Georgetown.

In this posed photograph, a woman pours alcohol from a walking stick at a soda fountain. *Courtesy of the Library of Congress.*

The liquor was being held as evidence in a case against two men who had been arrested in Lewes. The prosecution feared that the theft of what the *Sunday Star* called "casket polish" would destroy the case, since it was believed the thieves had swallowed the proof. According to the newspaper, "If rumhounds don't have any respect for the cellar of the law," bemoaned a former "mahogany decorator," his jaw beginning to quiver, "I'd like to ask what chance has poor guys like us got."[69]

The authorities had their hands full with policing Prohibition when the Ku Klux Klan reared its hooded head. Formed after the Civil War, the Klan harnessed the American racial animosities to attempt to counter the Fourteenth and Fifteenth Amendments to the Constitution, which attempted to guarantee Black Americans the rights of citizenship, particularly the right to vote. Using fear and intimidation, the Klan whipped and lynched, either by hanging or burning at the stake, anyone who dared to cross them. Suppressed in the late nineteenth century, the Klan experienced a resurgence before World War I. Delaware, a slave state, did not join the Confederacy, but after the Civil War, Jim Crow was alive and well in Delaware. Schools, theaters and other public places were segregated. Although the Klan was known for its anti-Black, anti-Jewish, anti-Catholic and anti-immigrant stands, the organization was also anti-alcohol and firmly supported Prohibition. In September 1921, the Klan came to Wilmington.

The first signs that a meeting of the Klan was taking place in Elsmere on the west edge of Wilmington were the sounds of rustling leaves, crackling of small twigs and the low buzz of voices in the woods near Union Street. Nearby residents noticed a number of cars arriving and notified police, who quickly dispersed the meeting without incident. Wilmington Klan kleagle R.S. Woolford, the Wilmington organizer of the "Invisible Empire Knights of the Ku Klux Klan," denied that the night meeting in the Elsmere woods was a secret session. He claimed that the forty men at the gathering were there to learn the details of the organization and that he was about to conclude the "open forum" he was conducting when the police arrived.[70] "We thought we were outside the city limits," Woolford said. The kleagle added, "We are going to have another information meeting some night next week, at which there will be present 175 men who desire to learn further particulars about the Klan, its purposes, requirements and the manner in which it conducts its affairs."[71]

The next day, a note was slipped under the door of Lancey Seeney, a Black resident of Carpenter Street. The note had a crude drawing of a skull and crossbones and the message, "Quit bootlegging. If you don't, you will be tarred and feathered at the telegraph pole at Fifth and Madison streets—KKK."[72] Seeney had every reason to be afraid. In the not-too-distant past, in June 1903, George White, a Black farmworker, was accused of the rape and murder of Helen Bishop, an eighteen-year-old White girl. White was arrested and jailed in the New Castle County Workhouse near Wilmington, where he was to be held until the Delaware courts ended their summer recess and he could be tried.[73] On Sunday, June 21, a throng of three thousand people attended an inflammatory sermon by the Reverend

In this editorial cartoon, the Anti-Saloon League swears allegiance to the Ku Klux Klan. *Courtesy of the Library of Congress.*

Robert A. Elwood, the pastor of Olivet Presbyterian Church, during which he rhetorically asked:

> *Should the murderer of Miss Bishop be lynched? Yes, but only under one condition, and that is this: if his trial shall be delayed until September, and then, though he be proven guilty, through some technicality of law or any undue influence upon either judges or jury, he be not given capital punishment, then the citizens of the state should arise in their might an execute the criminal and thus uphold the majesty of the law.*[74]

The day after Reverend Elwood's sermon, several thousand people, some of whom were well-dressed and carried umbrellas to protect themselves from the light rain, descended on the workhouse and dragged White to a nearby stack of wood and straw. After White had been shackled to a stake, the fire was ignited, and as he struggled in vain to escape the flames, his last words were, "Mercy, master, mercy." As White was consumed by the flames, some of the gentlemen in the crowd politely stepped aside so that the ladies could get a better view of the lynching. As the crowd slowly dispersed and the fire cooled, souvenir hunters sifted through the issues for pieces of George White's bones to take home as keepsakes.[75]

In 1921, when Seeney received the threatening note from the Klan accusing him of being a bootlegger, he dismissed the threat as a joke.

> *Sure it's got a skull and crossbones on it. The crossbones are just like soup bones. I ain't bootlegging. Why, I can scarcely get a drink for myself these days, and any man who would hire me to bootleg liquor for him would be taking an awful chance of my drinking it all. It's a joke played by some of my friends. They're trying to kid me.....No, I ain't worried about it a bit.[76]*

The beliefs of the Klan about Prohibition were not shared by many residents of Delaware, who tacitly supported the bootleggers. On the federal level, such support frustrated those who were charged with enforcing the Volstead Act. In the beginning of January 1921, federal agents began pushing to make the country "bone dry" in 1921, but the liquor continued to flow from homemade stills and from across the American border. According to the *Sunday Morning Star*, federal agents claimed, "Liquor is being smuggled into the U.S. from Canada, Mexico and Cuba. 1,000,000 quarts have been seized, but it is estimated that is one-tenth that gets across the borders."[77]

In Delaware, a stiff drink was still available in 1921, as W. Truxton Boyce, the federal Prohibition director for the state, knew well. In May, Boyce had heard persistent rumors that a shoeshine shop on West Second Street in Wilmington was operating as a front for bootleg liquor sales. Disguising himself as one of Wilmington's rougher residents, Boyce, accompanied by an informer who Boyce refused to name in order to protect him, went to the shoeshine that was operated by Harvey Kane. Boyce told the Wilmington *Evening Journal*, "When my companion and I reached the palace, we found Kane lounging outside. Approaching him, I asked if he could get a drink. He looked us over, nodded and said, 'Come on in.'" The three men went

Above: The crew of the Coast Guard cutter *Seneca* prepares to capture a rumrunner. *Courtesy of the Library of Congress.*

Right: A crewman from the *Seneca* takes aim at a bootlegger. *Courtesy of the Library of Congress.*

in through the shoeshining room to a back room. Boyce told Kane that he wanted to buy a half-pint of liquor, but Kane shook his head and said that no one could take any liquor out of the store unless it was in his stomach. Kane went on, "I don't intend to let any evidence be carried out of his place." Boyce replied, "All right. Give us a drink, then."[78]

Kane put out two whiskey glasses, got a bottle and filled them. Boyce took his glass and covered it with the palm of his hand and announced, "I am a federal officer, and you are under arrest." Without the slightest hesitation, Kane swung at Boyce's head with the whiskey bottle, but he parried the bottle with his arm. As Boyce drew his revolver, his companion ran into the street, shouting for the police.[79]

A policeman rushed into the room, and Boyce told him who he was. When the officer demanded identification, Boyce was flummoxed when he discovered that he had left his papers at the Prohibition Office, where he had put on his disguise. "Well," Boyce told the policeman, "suppose you take us both to the police station. That'll settle it." The bootlegger and the federal agent were put into a police wagon and taken to the station, where associates of Boyce identified him.[80]

Boyce said that, as a federal Prohibition director, it was not his business to enforce the laws against bootlegging, as that duty belonged to the regular federal enforcement officers. But he said that as long as there was an insufficient number of agents to properly enforce the Volstead Act, he believed that it was his duty, personally, to assist in suppressing illegal liquor traffic by any means.[81] By July 1921, Boyce had had enough of suppressing bootleg traffic and resigned his post to enter politics. Delaware was still far from "bone dry."

Smokey Hollow Raid

I don't believe whisky is being run to either the Jersey or Delaware Coasts.
—W.J. Burbage, Lewes shipping agent

The production of alcoholic drinks, wine, beer and distilled liquor involved gathering raw materials, a fermentation process and time. Wine is created when fruit, mostly grapes, is allowed to ferment without much human interference. The process, however, takes months, and Delaware bootleggers could not wait for mother nature to produce drinkable wine.

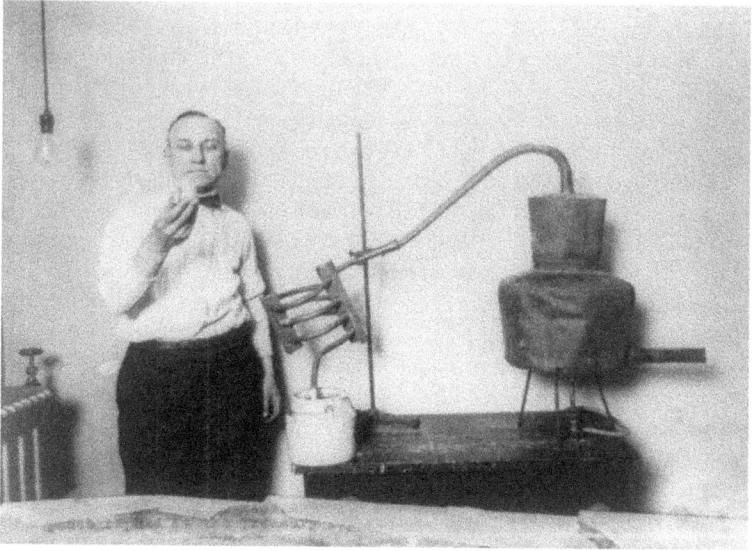

A man poses with a homemade still. *Courtesy of the Library of Congress.*

During Prohibition, most of the wine that was drunk in Delaware was either imported or from privately held stocks that had been acquired before the Eighteenth Amendment was passed. The brewing of beer was a quicker process than creating vintage wine. Tony Russo in *Delaware Beer: The Story of Brewing in the First State*, declared, "Simply put, beer is made by boiling the sugar out of malted barley, adding yeast and waiting."[82]

According to Garrett Peck in *Prohibition in Washington, D.C.: How Dry We Weren't*, "Thanks to the legions of German immigrants, beer became the nation's most popular alcoholic beverage after the Civil War."[83] Brewing beer did not take as much time as wine, but it took longer than distilling spiritous liquor, and the overwhelming majority of Delaware moonshiners set up stills to produce rum, the generic name for distilled liquor. According to Eric Mills in *Chesapeake Rumrunners of the Roaring Twenties*, "The basic still setup is simple....There's the main boiler kettle, called the 'cooker,' or 'can.' In here is the grain—cornmeal, rye, barely, whatever—mixed with distilled water, sugar, and though purist would argue, but expediency would dictate, yeast to cause fermentation."[84] This mixture, called "mash," was allowed to ferment for a few days and then heated at a low temperature to allow the alcohol to boil off. The alcoholic vapor is condensed in a coil encased in cold

Left: Stills came in all shapes and sizes. *Courtesy of the Library of Congress.*

Below: Delaware law enforcement agents confiscate a still that was hidden in southern Delaware. *Courtesy of the Delaware Public Archives.*

water to produce the liquid spirits.[85] The process was quicker than brewing beer or producing wine. Stills were small enough to be hidden in a basement in Wilmington, but most of the larger stills were set up on farms in the rural areas of Delaware.

In March 1922, federal Prohibition enforcement agents in Wilmington were gathering evidence against several men who were suspected of operating illegal stills in Sussex County. A fifty-gallon still had been discovered in the northern part of the county, and three men had been arrested and convicted of making illegal alcohol.[86] In spite of this arrest, the agents believed that the moonshining activities continued. Although hard evidence was understandably hard to obtain, by August, the agents had enough evidence to act. Gathering a mixed force of federal and state detectives and deputies, the agents set out for Wilmington in the middle of the night. Unfortunately, someone in cahoots with the moonshiners spotted the agents leaving the city. The tipster hopped into a car and headed south. At that time, the Du Pont Boulevard had not been completed as far as Wilmington, and the roads were of questionable quality. The agents had no reason to hurry, but the bootleg Paul Revere rushed south on the rutted roads to warn the moonshiners that the agents were coming.

At 4:00 a.m., the agents crossed into Sussex County, and when they reached the first of several places where the detectives suspected that distilleries were operating, they found nothing. The agents pressed on to a farm in the Smokey Hollow area of northern Sussex County, where an illegal still had been found in March and where the detectives had discovered two fifteen-gallon stills in the woods. The agents destroyed four hundred gallons of mash and took five gallons of whiskey, a large charcoal still burner, a large quantity of sugar and meal and arrested Pierce Traitor, a tenant farmer, who the agents believed was one of the most resourceful distillers in lower Delaware.[87]

Sweeping through the forest near Ellendale, the agents found six stills (one that had a fifty-gallon capacity), five hundred gallons of mash and a large quantity of whiskey and beer. Several arrests were made, including that of John J. Fortes, whom the Wilmington *Sunday Morning Star* described as, allegedly, "one of the biggest bootleggers in the county."[88]

In addition to the numerous stills that were hidden in the forests and swamps of Sussex County, bootleggers crossed into Delaware from the state's long border with Maryland. The boundary line between the two states ran through rural areas where the population was sparse and the support of bootleggers was strong. Unlike Delaware, where the Loose Law and the Klair

Law strengthened the Volstead Act, Maryland was the only state not to pass state legislation to support the local enforcement of Prohibition, earning it the nickname the "Free State."[89] Israel Howard, the chief enforcement officer of the Federal Prohibition Office, commented:

> *Delaware lies in what might be termed the very heart of a liquor belt. It is doubtful if there are two wetter cities to be found than Philadelphia and Baltimore; one to the north, and the other to the south of us. Then Delaware is not so far distant from New York as not to feel the effects of the liquor traffic there. And alongside of us is New Jersey, commonly regarded as none too dry.*[90]

Rumrunning vessels also deposited their illicit cargoes on the bay and ocean coasts of Southern Delaware.

The evidence of the moonshine stills on land was hard to deny, and no one doubted the existence of rumrunners who deposited their cargo at night and vanished as the booze was trucked to speakeasies. "I don't believe whisky is being run to either the Jersey or Delaware coasts," W.J. Burbage, a Lewes shipping agent, told the Philadelphia *Evening Public Ledger* in July 1921, "What would be the object of skippers bringing it so far north, with all the attendant risk, when they can find as ready a market nearer the Bahamas, on our southern coast?" The Philadelphia newspaper added, "The Lewes Methodist minister, the Rev. Mr. Davis, says that after an investigation extending over two years, he is convinced likewise that there is no rumrunning in Delaware." Despite the protestations of Burbage and Davis, in the second year of Prohibition, the Delaware sands were being littered with empty Jamaica rum and whisky bottles.[91]

Almost as soon as Prohibition began, rumrunners began to use the isolated beaches of the southern Delaware Coast to land illicit booze. Starting in the Bahamas or Canada, rumrunners arrived off the Delaware Coast, where they remained in international waters, safe from the interference of American law enforcement officials. After nighfall, the illegal alcohol was loaded into small boats for the final run to the beach, where the bootleggers would reload the booze onto trucks that would carry the illegal alcohol to speakeasies in Washington, D.C.; Baltimore; and Philadelphia.

Despite the assertion by some coastal residents that no illegal alcohol was being landed on the Delaware Coast, rumors persisted that the area between the inlet and Fenwick Island was a favorite landing spot for bootleg booze. The navy sent several seaplanes to assist the ground patrols. According to the

During Prohibition, the coast of southern Delaware at Fenwick Island was undeveloped, giving rumrunners an inviting place to land their booze. *Courtesy of the Delaware Public Archives.*

Evening Public Ledger, "Two big and powerful navy seaplanes came ranging over the sands of Bethany Beach, [Delaware], flying not more than sixty feet above the sand dunes. The men in the cockpits of the big 'boats' waved a greeting as they sped by."[92] As the vacationers on the beaches watched, the newspaper reported:

> *For a few minutes, the roar of the Liberty engines shattered the air and then slowly merged with the roar of the ocean as the big craft became specks on the horizon. The planes were flying in the direction of the Delaware Bay. They were on the "rum patrol." It is one of the new jobs of the navy fliers, made more important now with much talk of whisky running along the Delaware Coast.*[93]

The *Evening Public Ledger* noted that coastal residents had different opinions on whether illegal alcohol was landed on the Delaware Coast or not, but the newspaper also reported:

If it means anything, on a six-mile walk over the wind-swept sands and through the dunes of this wild bit of seaboard, twenty-three empty Jamaica rum and whiskey bottles were counted. And strewn along the beach also were green bananas, such as are washed or tossed overboard from boats sailing from tropical islands of the South. It would be hard to find a better place for the running in of contraband cargoes than this wild stretch in the neighborhood of Bethany Beach, where stories of rum smuggling have been rife.[94]

Although some coastal residents continued to believe that rumrunners were not landing their illegal cargoes on Delaware beaches, the empty rum and whiskey bottles told another tale.

In August 1921, Robert B. Elliott, the newly appointed Prohibition director for Delaware, and several members of his staff made an inspection tour of Sussex County, and they reported that there was considerably more talk than actual bootlegging in Southern Delaware. They denied that there were many stills in the lower part of the state. Although not much hard liquor was being made in that part of the state, the *Evening Journal* reported, "The officers did find, however, that many citizens in the county were making their own beer and wine for home consumption."[95] Director Elliott had a lot to learn.

Small sailboats carrying illegal hooch could navigate Delaware waters quietly. *Courtesy of the Delaware Public Archives.*

By Land and Sea

Of course, there are some stills in the city.
—George Black, Wilmington Police superintendent

"There was no little laughter today about the city, some of it in high places," the *Evening Journal* reported, "over the declaration of a New York newspaper that Delaware is the driest state in the union and, more particularly, that 'just one gallon of illegal whiskey was seized in the past year in the state' and that 'no stills were taken and but fifty-two gallons of beer.'"[96] With the blatantly false report in hand, an *Evening Journal* reporter scampered over to Prohibition director Elliott to demand a summary of the work that had been done by his office. He obligingly reported that, in the past six months, his office had made twenty-eight arrests for unlawful liquor transportation, sale or possession, resulting in thirteen convictions, with fifteen cases still pending. Ten stills were seized, 590 gallons of mash were destroyed and 159 gallons of finished product were captured. New Castle County, including Wilmington, led the three Delaware counties with twenty arrests. The other eight were in Sussex County, and no arrests were made in Kent County. On the other hand, six stills were destroyed in Sussex County—twice the number the federal agents had found in New Castle County. Just one still was discovered in Kent County. The *Evening Journal* explained Sussex's dominance in stills, saying it was due to "the practice in lower Delaware of distilling 'corn likker' or 'white mule,' as it is known."[97]

Superintendent of Police Black pointed out that 498 arrests for drunkenness were made in the previous fiscal year, as opposed to 294 the year before. Superintendent Black said:

> *How can you prevent a man from going only fifteen miles from Wilmington, above the state line, and getting all the intoxicants he wants. That is where a lot our trouble develops. Of course, there are some stills in the city, but they are in private homes, and their owners make liquor for their own use. They do not sell any of it, which makes it extremely difficult to get any evidence against them. On the whole, I think we have a pretty clean city.*[98]

There was another indication that bootlegging in Delaware was not solely the work of outsiders, according to the *Evening Journal* in March 1922, "One official, in speaking of the great increase in drunkenness here during the past two weeks, estimated that there were at least two thousand stills, most of them in homes in operation in this city at the present time."[99] There were increased sales of copper tanks and tubing. The variety of "hooch," which the *Evening Journal* reported appeared to be of a "fighting brand," led to a number of street brawls. One of the most serious fights occurred at Fifth and Lombard Streets, where a crowd of White men who had been drinking attacked a Black man who dared to dance past them on the street. The Black man was knocked unconscious with a brick, and his friends took up the fight. Hundreds of bricks were tossed, and the sidewalk was spattered with blood.[100]

Although cars were becoming more and more dependable, breakdowns were common, and motorists belonged to an unspoken fraternity and often assisted other drivers in need. In April 1922, federal agents faked a breakdown on the busy Philadelphia Pike in the hopes of nabbing a bootlegger. Sure enough, a car with three men stopped to help, and the police arrested the good Samaritans after whiskey was found in their car. A few days later, the situation was reversed. Two federal agents and an official from the Anti-Saloon League were in New Castle at 2:00 a.m. when they came across four men whose car was having engine trouble. While inspecting the car, ostensibly, to see what was wrong, the agents discovered five gallons of liquor. The agents announced that the four men were under arrest, and all hell broke loose. One man started to run. The agents fired several shots into the air to make him stop. The others in the car also began to flee, and as they did so, several bootleggers pulled out their guns, and a brief gun battle ensued. Afterward, the bootleggers surrendered. The four men were arrested, the agents managed to start the broken-down car and the entire party drove to Wilmington.[101]

As the highjacking of the gin from Chester indicated, some hooch was shipped down the river Delaware River from the Philadelphia area, and at the other end of the state, suspected rumrunning vessels were spotted lurking off the Delaware Coast. In November 1921, a British schooner was spotted lurking in international waters. Customs officials boarded the sailing vessel and questioned the skipper. He freely admitted that he had fifteen thousand cases of scotch on board, but he insisted that his destination was Halifax in Canada. Because he was beyond the three-mile limit off the coast, the agents could do nothing. It is not known whether he landed any of the alcohol in Delaware.[102]

There was no doubt, Philadelphia officials believed, that large quantities of liquor were being smuggled up the Delaware River in small, unobtrusive craft. A. Lincoln Acker, the customs collector of the Port of Philadelphia,

Large schooners were often used as motherships that remained off the coast while they unloaded their illegal alcohol onto smaller vessels for the run to shore. *Courtesy of the Delaware Public Archives.*

remarked, "The rumrunners, who wear no cutlasses but have more effective Colt .45 automatic in ready reach, are as bold and defiant as were the buccaneers of colonial days, who hawked their stolen goods up Dock Creek and spent their blood-stained gold in the pot houses along the riverbank."[103] The contraband was being brought in on all types of ships—on regular freight and passenger service boats and tramp steamers. According to reports, these oceangoing ships brought anywhere from three hundred to seven hundred cases of choice liquor each. The overseas agents who acted for local bootleggers purchased the liquor with the connivance of the captains or other ship's officers. A meeting point was sent by radio and code to the bootleggers, and when the ship reached the Delaware Breakwater at Lewes, the captain slowed the ship's engines to allow a flotilla of small boats to rendezvous with the ship. The cases of liquor were then tossed overboard. The buoyant cases were easily fished out by the small boats and run ashore, where there were several convenient landing spots on the Delaware side of the bay. The liquor was then cached in a secure hiding spot or immediately transferred to trucks to complete the last leg of the bootlegging journey.

A Prohibition cartoon in which one man asks, "How big is she?" The other man answers, "About 50 cases." *Courtesy of the Library of Congress.*

Acker believed that the only effective method of combating these rumrunners was using fast boats crewed by customs officers, "who will draw as ready an automatic [pistol] at their foes."[104]

Liquor was not carried aboard American ships surreptitiously; rather, it was carried openly. The United States Shipping Board, which had been established during World War I to oversee American merchant and passenger ships, maintained that carrying liquor and serving it to passengers was entirely legal. That practice prompted August A. Busch, the president of Anheuser-Busch, to charge that these ships were in violation of the Volstead Act, making the United States government "the greatest bootlegger in the world."[105]

Shipping board chairman Albert Lasker answered that as long as the ships were beyond the three-mile limit, the Volstead Act did not apply. He believed that American ships could not compete with foreign vessels if they did not serve liquor. According to Lasker, "So long as Great Britain, Japan, France, Germany and other maritime nations continue to serve liquors to American passengers, there [are] a sufficient number of Americans without proper pride in their own flagships who would divert their trade to the foreign flags." Lasker claimed that Busch wanted to create a public revolt against Prohibition in order to revive his brewery. Lasker also echoed the anti-German feelings that were prevalent during World War I:

> *It is, of course, notorious that Adolphus Busch, who founded your brewery, was possibly the Kaiser's closest friend in America and that your family, for many years, has maintained a castle in Germany; your action in any event will not displease your German friends whose greatest hope of a restored German merchant marine is a hurt to America's new-born merchant marine.*[106]

DON'T RETURN

It was one of the crudest that has yet been found by the "hooch hounds."
It is said to have been made from a five-gallon kerosene can.
—Evening Journal

By November 1921, it was obvious that the Prohibition agents needed more weapons if they were truly going to make Delaware dry. Federal agents were deputized as collectors of internal revenue. Although this strategy would eventually bring down Al Capone, some Delaware newspapers were not having it. Some government officials believed that there were twenty-five or thirty bootleggers in Wilmington who made false returns and who owed millions of dollars in back taxes. The *Wilmington Daily Commercial* editorialized:

> *If these men have made fortunes by defying the United States law, and if the Department of Justice can prove it, the business is to put the men in jail and not to be bothering them about income taxes. Of course, the fact that the department can't prove any such thing, but some of its attorneys hope to prove that these men have made a lot of money somehow or other…under the assumption that the money came from bootlegging, they may be able to collect income taxes on some of it.*[107]

Using the tax law to stop bootlegging in the state did not make Delaware dry.

While the dry agents wrestled with the urban bootleggers who had stills hidden in Wilmington homes, in the lower part of the state, the oceanside resort of Rehoboth Beach dealt with a different sort of illegal whiskey. By the start of Prohibition, the resort had grown into a fashionable vacation spot that attracted a cosmopolitan crowd of visitors from Washington, D.C., and had earned the title of the "Nation's Summer Capital." During the winter months, the crowds disappeared, and Rehoboth's population was reduced to a few hundred permanent residents. With the beaches deserted, there was room for rumrunners to land their liquor and for stills to operate. In January 1922, federal agents made a sweep of coastal Sussex County and discovered four stills and a pair of sportily attired moonshiners. Federal Agent Edwards, assisted by State Detective Ottie Donaway and Deputy Royman were searching a wooded area between Lewes and Rehoboth Beach. While working their way through thickets so dense that, sometimes, they needed to cut away the undergrowth to clear their path, the agents

Rehoboth was considered the nation's summer capital because it was popular with government officials. *Courtesy of the Delaware Public Archives.*

located an elaborate distilling operation of four interconnected fifteen-gallon stills. One was fired up and running, and another appeared to be ready to be started. One huge coil was shared by the four stills, and they were set up so that at least one still was going at all times. Although they were connected by the coil, the stills were spaced in the thick underbrush far enough away from each other that only one was visible at a time. As the agents were uncovering the stills, they encountered two teenagers, Dan Schimer and Jack Wolf, who were dressed in white flannels, white sport shirts, yachting caps and nifty white shoes. When Agent Edwards approached the two nattily dressed young men, he asked Wolf, "What's your name?" Wolf stood there, silent, and then Schimer spoke up, and with a bow to the agents, he said, "And I am Dan Schimer, known as Gentleman Dan." The talkative Gentleman Dan then took off running. The agents shouted for him to stop, and when he ignored this warning, Agent Edwards drew his revolver from his pocket. Taking aim at the fleeing Schimer, Edwards fired a single shot. The bullet knocked the yachting cap from Schimer's head, and the young moonshiner needed no further persuasion to surrender. The two "gentlemen moonshiners" were arrested, and three of the four stills, along with most of the whiskey, were destroyed. The four stills and two gallons of whiskey were seized as evidence.[108] These two young men, who were described as "little more than boys," were later arraigned in court, lectured and paroled. One of the teenagers resumed his bootlegging ways and was arrested again. That time, he provided the Prohibition agents with valuable information that resulted in the roundup of those who were involved in landing illicit booze at Lewes, where the rumrunners were planning to make the town of Cape Henlopen a base for importing booze from offshore motherships.[109] The *Evening Journal* reported, "With the arrest of two sportily attired youths and capture of four stills, federal prohibition agents believed they have cut off a leading source of wet goods supplied to summer resorts in lower Delaware and Maryland."[110]

While the Prohibition agents may have put a dent in moonshining in Southern Delaware, they did not stop it. In March 1922, a squad of agents posing as umbrella menders made their way across the western part of Sussex County. During the 1920s, it was common to see itinerant knife sharpeners, umbrella menders and other craftsmen plying the streets of small towns with portable workbenches slung over their backs, ringing bells and calling out their skills. The disguised agents aroused little suspicion as they traipsed up and down the roads, watching for any sign of an illegal still or other bootlegging activity. Two miles east of Laurel, the agents discovered a crude still and arrested a tenant farmer. According to the *Evening Journal*, "It was one of the crudest that has yet been found by the 'hooch hounds.' It is said to have been made from a five-gallon kerosene can. It is claimed by the officers that the products of a still of this kind are poisonous, the lead from the sides of the can dissolving into the liquid when heated, a deadly lead poison resulting."[111] The booze from this still was suspected to be the cause of death in the case of Noah Collins. In March 1921, the seventy-six-year-old Collins died, according to the Wilmington newspaper *Every Evening*, "as a result of imbibing too freely of Lower Delaware 'hooch,' commonly called 'corn stock buck.'" Harry Lynch of Roxana, a small crossroads town in Baltimore Hundred, was charged with manslaughter for supplying the "hooch," but the Sussex County grand jury refused to indict him.[112]

The agents continued to gather evidence, and a month later, a mixed force of federal, state and local detectives gathered in Laurel and set out to clear Southern Delaware of moonshiners. After raiding farms near Williamsville, Selbyville and Millsboro, where they found one still and other evidence of bootlegging activity, the grouped turned its attention to Byron Lynch's farm near Roxana.[113] On Lynch's property, the agents discovered a large moonshining operation consisting of a "king" still of more than a one-hundred-gallon capacity with a ⅜-inch copper coil that could turn out a gallon of rye or peach brandy every fifteen minutes. This giant still, with its huge brick furnace, was reputedly known throughout the lower part of Delaware as the "Old Lunch Burner." The still was hidden in the woods, not far from the house of Frank Wells, who stood nearby as the dry agents closed in the "Old Lunch Burner." As Wells, an acquaintance of Lynch's, watched, Lynch suddenly appeared, running from the woods and firing a pistol. Lynch did not aim at the detectives; instead, he shot five times at Wells, who Lynch thought had ratted out the location of the still. As the detectives scattered for cover, Lynch went into Wells's house and attempted to set it on fire. During the confusion, Lynch's brother, Charles, drove up in a car. In his frenzy, Byron fired at him, but he quickly recognized his brother. He then hopped into the car, and the two men drove off a short distance.[114]

By then, other moonshiners had gathered in the woods around the "Old Lunch Burner," and they opened fire on the detectives. The moonshiners were well-hidden, and at first, the detectives refrained from returning fire. After sundown, when the gun flashes revealed the locations of the shooters, the firing on both sides became general. An intermittent barrage continued for some time until the dry officers were able to drive the moonshiners away from the underbrush and into a swampy area. As the detectives continued to advance into the wetlands, they had to wade through knee-deep water. After midnight, both sides settled down for an all-night siege, and several detectives were sent to a nearby town to secure food. Sporadic firing continued on both sides, but after daybreak, the shooting ceased. When the detectives emerged from their cover, they discovered that the moonshiners had slipped away in the dark. None of the detectives had been injured. If any of the moonshiners had been hit, they were able to slip away despite their injuries.[115] No arrests were made as a result of this raid, but a little more than two weeks later, a dry detective was driving through Baltimore Hundred, looking for suspicious activity, when he stopped for lunch in one of the small towns that dot the landscape of Southern Delaware. After finishing his meal, he returned to his car and found his tires slashed and a scrawled-out note on the seat that said in large letters, "Don't return."[116]

3

RISE OF THE RUMRUNNERS

RICH HOOCH HARVEST ON THE DELAWARE RIVER

Of course, we are aware of rum smuggling here…but we are handicapped and utterly unable to cope with the situation.
—*J.H. Lathy, assistant customs collector for Philadelphia*

Wilmington, Delaware, was long the older, smaller stepchild of Philadelphia, Pennsylvania. Established by the Swedes almost a half century before William Penn founded his "City of Brotherly Love," Wilmington remained a small river town as Philadelphia grew into one of America's largest metropolitan areas. At the beginning of Prohibition, Wilmington had grown to a sizable city, with over 100,000 residents within its borders and another one hundred thousand in the surrounding area. The Wilmington area contained more than half of the state's population, and the city was a behemoth compared to the next largest Delaware town, Dover, the state's capital, which had a paltry population of less than five thousand. In the early 1920s, Wilmington embarked on a major construction project to build a modern marine terminal to siphon off some of Philadelphia's seagoing business. When the new facility opened in May 1923, the Wilmington *Sunday Morning Star* gushed, "With a long and honorable history in the past—from the time when the Swedes first landed to carve homes for themselves in the New World wilderness, on down through the Revolutionary period and the late century—Wilmington, Delaware, stands today on the threshold of a new era."[117]

Wilmington's booming waterfront catered to vessels from around the world. *Courtesy of the Delaware Public Archives.*

The new $3 million marine terminal was situated on over two hundred acres, much of it reclaimed marshland, on the south bank of the Christina River, at its junction with the Delaware River. A 1,210-foot-long wharf on the Christina River could accommodate three modern cargo ships at once. A giant forty-ton electric crane ran on rails that extended the entire length of the wharf; it facilitated the unloading of cargo, work that was once done by gangs of stevedores assisted by hand-powered winches, pulleys and ropes. The cargo could be stored in several large warehouses, or it could be loaded immediately onto trains. The terminal had enough track that if it were placed end-to-end, it would reach from Wilmington to Philadelphia. With the construction of the marine terminal, Wilmington, according to the *Sunday Morning Star*, was the "Queen City of the Delmarva Peninsula."[118]

Wilmington's new marine terminal successfully attracted ships that may have otherwise docked at Philadelphia, and along with the legal cargo, some of these ships carried illicit booze. In May 1923, A. Lincoln Acker, the customs collector of the Port of Philadelphia, repeated his call for small cutters to combat the fleet boats that were reaping a rich hooch harvest on the Delaware River between Wilmington and Philadelphia. Acker made several visits to Washington to meet with U.S. Treasury Department officials, during which he argued for a well-manned cutter to drive the smugglers from the "Rum

Row" that bootleggers had established on the river. Acker was turned down. The U.S. Navy Department refused to transfer a cutter that Acker had in mind, and Acker had no money to purchase it outright. In addition, treasury department officials said that they had no funds for the upkeep of such a vessel. J.H. Lathy, the assistant customs collector, remarked, "Of course, we are aware of rum smuggling here. We couldn't very well help being aware of it, but we are handicapped and utterly unable to cope with the situation without a boat to pursue the speedy craft which the smugglers are using."[119]

Federal authorities estimated that, at that time, liquor from foreign ports was being delivered into places along the Delaware River, like Wilmington and Philadelphia, more than any other time since the beginning of Prohibition. During the last week of May 1923, forty foreign ships, a new record for maritime arrivals from ports, came up the Delaware River. Some of these vessels were modern steamships with contraband liquor cargoes stashed below deck, and others were dingy sailing ships with foc'sles that were well-stocked with hooch.[120]

When Wilmington updated its port facilities to service modern steam-powered merchant ships, the age of sailing was in its final days. By the late nineteenth century, most new ships were powered by steam. Some shipowners, however, discovered that sailing schooners could be more efficient for shorter coastal trips. To keep the number of crew members to a minimum, vessels were rigged with sails that were attached directly to three or four masts that could be handled by two or three men from the schooner's deck. In the late nineteenth century, small shipyards in Milford, Milton, Laurel, Bethel and elsewhere turned out moderate-sized sailing vessels that some bootleggers found to be ideal for the surreptitious cruises. The larger schooners, the supply or motherships, were mostly fishing schooners, whose low freeboard (the distance between the water and the top deck) enabled fish to be hauled aboard more easily, and they were able to carry one thousand to three thousand cases on a single trip. Before they were converted into rumrunners, these workman-like schooners sailed through heavy seas in search of the catch. Without engine noise to alert the Coast Guard and without telltale smoke to leave a trail to follow, rumrunning schooners anchored just outside of the three-mile limit, where they were clearly visible from shore. They attracted a motley collection of small motorboats and, occasionally, rowboats filled with thirsty people eager to buy bootleg liquor.[121]

A number of suspected bootlegging schooners were seen lurking off Cape Henlopen, like the British schooner that had a cargo of fifteen thousand cases of scotch and was allegedly bound for Halifax that was discovered off the

Delaware coast in November 1921. Almost a year after that incident, Robert B. Elliott, the federal director of Prohibition for Delaware, announced, "The intensive war waged upon violators during the past month has forced the majority of illicit dealers, especially smugglers in this state to seek more lucrative fields."[122] Elliott went on to claim that, at that time, his office was receiving fewer complaints about illegal booze and rumrunners than at any other time since Prohibition began. Elliott did concede that the rumrunners and bootleggers would attempt to ramp up their activities in September and October, but recent efforts had "an almost blanketing effect, and any new turn of affairs on part of bootleggers will make little headway." He went on to say that those who support Prohibition should feel optimistic that the laws against alcohol would be strictly enforced. Elliott claimed, "We have few complaints today than perhaps at any time in the history of this office. Things are pronouncedly quiet throughout the state, and there is practically no rumrunning traffic along the Delaware Coast."[123]

A month after Elliott declared that there was no rumrunning along the coast, residents of Rehoboth Beach spotted a suspicious schooner anchored off the beach. During the 1920s, Rehoboth was strictly a summer resort, and during the fall, there were very few people in town. Rehoboth and the small community of Dewey Beach were surrounded by acres of unspoiled beaches that provided dark and quiet landing places for bootleggers. At night, the sailing vessel was apparently transferring bootleg liquor to small motor boats that ran ashore with their precious cargo. After the small boats landed, the booze was picked up by trucks, which sped off to complete the delivery. By the time Prohibition agents were notified, the schooner, the small boats and the illicit cargo were gone.[124]

I'M NOT SO BAD

Bootlegging thrives because there are citizens who encourage it.
—Robert Elliott, federal director of Prohibition for Delaware

In the first few years of Prohibition, the mobsters had not yet taken control of the rumrunning traffic, and much of the bootlegging was done by otherwise law-abiding citizens. Many residents of Delaware supported Prohibition in order to rid the state of the raucous corner saloons, where excessive drinking and bawdy behavior were common. A number of voters

Lewes on the bay side of Cape Henlopen was popular with tourists and rumrunners. *Courtesy of the Delaware Public Archives.*

who supported Prohibition had always enjoyed a cold beer or a glass of wine with their meals, and suddenly, that was illegal. Most Wilmington residents did not set up stills in their basements, but many of them knew which houses were producing hooch. On the coast, local watermen obeyed the law, but they also guided the rumrunners past the shoals and shallows that peppered Delaware Bay.

Located in the lee of Cape Henlopen, on the south side of the mouth of the bay, Lewes residents considered their town, the "first town in the first state." Although the first European settlement was established along Lewes Creek in 1631, that Dutch settlement was destroyed by Natives after a few months. By the time Europeans returned to the Cape Henlopen area, they had established other settlements farther up the Delaware. Nonetheless, the people of Lewes were proud of their heritage, and before Prohibition was over, they planned an extensive celebration for the three hundredth anniversary of the founding of the town.

Perched on the doorstep of Delaware Bay, some of the residents of Lewes developed a deep understanding of the shifting shallows and sand bars that peppered the bottom of the bay, and they became Delaware Bay and River pilots who helped guide ships past these underwater hazards. Tradition has it that the first pilot was a Native American. When Prohibition began, the deep-draft schooners and other large vessels would not dare to venture up the bay without the aid of a pilot, and few pilots would risk their reputations to guide a rumrunner up the bay. Consequently, the large motherships that anchored off the coast used smaller, faster, motor-driven boats to ferry their hooch ashore.

Although they may not have had pilots to guide them, there were a number of watermen who were familiar with the shoals and shallows. In the 1920s, there were several fish processing plants between Lewes and Cape Henlopen. These plants turned the oily menhaden fish into paint, fertilizer and other products. The plants were fed by a fleet of small fishing vessels manned by Lewes residents, some of whom opposed Prohibition and were all too happy to aid the bootleggers. In addition, there were several passive aids to navigation that the rumrunners could use to safely guide their way. The most prominent was the Cape Henlopen Lighthouse. A decade before the American Revolution, the merchants of Philadelphia financed the construction of the beacon that was constructed on a high dune about a quarter mile from the surf. When the granite tower was finished, the sturdy eight-sided lighthouse was over sixty-nine feet tall. During the night, the light from the beacon warned mariners away from the treacherous waters near the cape. During the day, the distinctive white tower served as an important landmark to legitimate captains and illegal bootleggers. In addition, there were a host of other aids. A smaller beacon stood near the tip of the cape, lighthouses marked the ends of the Delaware Breakwater and lightships were anchored over some of the more treacherous shoals. At the southern end of Delaware's ocean coast, the Fenwick Island Lighthouse provided another guiding light to mariners. The salty captains who sailed the rumrunning schooners knew these navigation aids, and they also knew not to venture too close to the three-mile limit, where they could run aground and be easy prey for the Prohibition agents.

Delaware director Elliott complained that bootleggers and rumrunners were successful because Delaware residents willingly paid high prices for bootleg booze.

> *Bootlegging thrives because there are citizens who encourage it. The people who patronize bootleggers today are not the poor and the ignorant. If the men of means who pay high prices for liquor should refuse to buy it, bootlegging would cease. It will never cease, however, while rich men and women continue to encourage bootlegging, rumrunning, smuggling and the violation.* [125]

Above: At the beginning of Prohibition, Cape Henlopen Lighthouse sat perilously close to the edge of a high dune. *Courtesy of the Delaware Public Archives.*

Opposite: Rumrunners battled the Coast Guard to bring their illicit booze ashore. *Courtesy of the Library of Congress.*

Ordinary people supported the bootleggers because of the deeply ingrained belief that not every drinker was a drunk and not every bootlegger was a crook. Although cold-hearted mobsters were behind some of the bootlegging operations, some rumrunners were personable, charismatic people, such as William McCoy, the reputed "King of the Rumrunners."[126]

Born in rural New York State, McCoy went to sea on a merchant ship when he was eighteen years old. Four years later, he stepped ashore to establish a yacht building business in Daytona Beach, Florida. When Prohibition began, McCoy acquired several schooners and began running whiskey from the Bahamas and the West Indies to locations along the Atlantic Coast. Tall, bronzed, wiry and extremely fit, McCoy looked much younger than his forty-something years. He frequented the Mid-Atlantic Coast aboard his rumrunning schooner, but it is not known whether he stopped along the Delaware Coast to unload his booze. It is known, however, that McCoy specialized in high-class liquor, and his booze became known as "the real McCoy," a term that denoted quality, which became part of the American lexicon.[127]

In December 1923, the Coast Guard cutter *Seneca* spotted McCoy and his booze-hauling schooner, *Tomoka*, off Seabright on the northern coast of New Jersey. After a brief chase, during which shots were fired, McCoy surrendered. When the bootlegger learned of a report that he offered the commander of the *Seneca* $2,000 to forget he had captured McCoy, the rumrunning captain said, "Do you know what I offered him: hot coffee and biscuits and an overcoat to keep from freezing." McCoy's capture effectively put an end to his rumrunning, and when he was caught, a reporter wrote, "Looks like a farmer, talks like a lawyer and has the eyes of a weather-beaten face of a sailor." McCoy smiled a friendly grin, "Oh, I'm not so bad."[128]

Many people in Delaware thought McCoy and other rumrunners were not so bad, and this made it difficult to compel people to comply with the liquor laws. The overlapping and inconsistent federal, state and local efforts to rid Delaware of intoxicating beverages also made prosecution of the Prohibition laws even more challenging. From the beginning of Prohibition, assistant secretary of the treasury Roy A. Haynes oversaw the federal agents who enforced the Volstead Act, and he was the civilian in charge of the Coast Guard that attempted to halt rumrunning on the coasts of the United States. By 1925, Haynes's work was seen as unorganized and ineffective, and he was replaced by retired general Lincoln C. Andrews. According to *Time* magazine, "[Andrews] took charge of Prohibition enforcement as a captain takes charge of a ship, purposed to navigate it like an old New England skipper. Finding that one of the chief obstacles in his way was his crew, he set out to remove it. Plans were laid, and last week, he announced that the weak must walk the plank and traitors hang from the yard arm."[129]

Andrews made a number of personnel changes to clear out enforcement agents who were "composed of one-part fanatics and one-part politicians." He claimed that some of these agents had secured their jobs "on the recommendation of politicians, of saloonkeepers, ex-bartenders and other wets has been shameful and, in some sections, almost to the exclusion of friends of the law."[130]

In a column published in the *Sunday Morning Star*, Andrews echoed John Paul Jones when the new director of federal Prohibition enforcement declared, "Our fight against rum smuggling has not yet begun." According to Andrews, the Coast Guard had only been "experimenting" with ways to stop rumrunning vessels from landing illegal booze on American coasts. Andrews contended that plans were being made to shut down the hooch traffic:

> *We have not yet completed our system for the gathering of information about the "enemy," but I can say that we expect effective cooperation from foreign governments, and we expect to put enough vessels on the coast to break up any more concentrated invasions of our coast lines. It will take time, but in the end, the government will win because it must win.*[131]

PRESIDENTIAL INTERLUDE

No president probably ever received a quieter welcome than the one Wilmington today gave Warren G. Harding.
—New York Times

As Prohibition rolled through its third year of bootleggers bringing their illegal hooch to market and law enforcement officials trying to stop them, both the state of Delaware and President Warren G. Harding needed a break. On Saturday, June 9, 1923, President Harding took a train from Washington, D.C., and arrived at noon in Wilmington, where he was met by a welcoming committee. His small entourage was taken to a line of waiting cars for the short drive to the Hotel Du Pont, where he had lunch with the Young Men's Republican Club. Crowds lined the route of the presidential motorcade, and the *Sunday Morning Star* reported, "The trip from the depot to the Hotel Du Pont was one continuous ovation, and kept the president busy in responding to the plaudits of the one of the largest crowds ever seen on Market Street."[132] On the other hand, the *New York Times* commented, "The president received everywhere a quiet and respectful getting. At Wilmington, where a crowd of 40,000 to 50,000 jammed the streets, the lack of cheering and handclapping was noted by everyone. No president probably ever received a quieter welcome than the one Wilmington today gave Warren G. Harding."[133]

During the lunch with the young Republicans, Harding made a short extemporaneous speech, during which the president lamented the growing isolationism in the United States. According to the *Sunday Morning Star*, he declared, "The United States cannot be happy if the rest of civilization were in constant distress....We don't just live by ourselves anymore."[134] The *New York Times* reported that the president confessed that he was unaware of some aspects of Delaware's history. "I did not know until today that Delaware was the first state to subscribe to the Union. I guess you were so small that you thought it would not hurt to do the right thing. It was a good thing."[135] The *New York Times* also pointed out, "The color line did not obtain at the luncheon to the president, for among those present were several negroes."[136] After declaring, "It is good to get out of Washington and breathe the good air of America," Harding's motorcade headed for Newark.[137] Traveling in an open car so that he would be visible to the crowds of people who lined the roads to cheer him, the presidential caravan slowed to a crawl. According to the

In 1923, spectators lined the streets of Milford to catch a glimpse of President Warren Harding. *Courtesy of the Delaware Public Archives.*

Wilmington Sunday Morning Star, "On request of Mrs. Harding, the speed of the motors was held down, and as the afternoon wore on, she showed signs of fatigue, though she bore up splendidly."[138]

At Newark, Harding briefly addressed a crowd in front of the Women's College, and then the presidential party reboarded the motorcade and headed south to Cooch's Bridge, the site of a battle during the American Revolution, during which the new American flag was reputedly flown for the first time in battle.[139] Harding's party halted briefly to read a bronze tablet that described the significance of Cooch's Bridge before moving south to Glasgow, where they passed a Civil War veteran, dressed in his faded blue uniform, holding his old army rifle at "present arms" to salute the president.[140]

As Harding's motorcade made its way south, the roads were lined with crowds that included school children who were waiting to get a peek at the chief executive. When the president's car passed by, the *New York Times* again reported that many of the children remained oddly silent as they waved small American flags.[141]

It was nearly 6:00 p.m. when the presidential party reached Milford, where an estimated crowd of twenty thousand people lined the streets to

As President Harding made his way through Delaware, he was welcomed by large, but sometimes quiet, crowds. *Courtesy of the Delaware Public Archives.*

get a glimpse of the president. Harding was scheduled to watch an Eastern Shore League baseball game, but he fell so far behind schedule that the president's car could only stop briefly at the ballfield and bow to the teams and spectators. After a stop for dinner, Harding was initiated into the Tall Cedars of Lebanon during a ceremony at the Plaza Theatre that took over two hours.[142]

It was nearing midnight when President Harding was loaded his car and his motorcade began driving to Lewes. According to the *New York Times*, "All the way from Milford...to Lewes, the road was lined with persons who had stood awaiting his coming from early in the evening. At Georgetown, Harbeson, and Cool Spring, the houses were illuminated, while the residents stood in the road waving lanterns and flags. In response to their cheers, the president and Mrs. Harding bowed and waved their hands."[143]

After rolling through the streets of Lewes, the presidential motorcade pulled up to the pier, where a small boat was waiting to take him to the presidential yacht, *Mayflower*, which was anchored behind the Delaware Breakwater. At the pier, Harding thanked the small crowd of people who had waited up nearly all night to see him, and the president assured them that the day had been one of the longest and most pleasant in his life.[144]

While in Milford, President Harding was inducted into the Tall Cedars of Lebanon at the Plaza Theatre. *Courtesy of the Delaware Public Archives.*

As the motorcade entered Sussex County and turned toward Lewes, the president could not quite free himself from the Washington political scene.

Harding left Lewes aboard the *Mayflower* around 3:00 a.m. to rendezvous with the seaplane that was carrying copies of the *New York Times*.[145] Having breathed the good air of America in Delaware, President Harding opened the newspaper and plunged back into the latest cloud of political incompetence. According to the *New York Times*:

> It was a great day for Delaware. To members of the president's party, it seemed as if a state holiday had been declared and the entire population of the commonwealth had crowded to the cities, the towns and the villages and along the roadsides to wave a greeting to the chief executive and the first lady as they passed by...some of the little towns, which never in their long history entertained a president.[146]

For Delaware and President Harding, the day had been a brief respite from the problems of Prohibition, which was not mentioned once in the president's reported remarks.

Dragon's Blood for Sale

Holy horrors! We'll have no more of the stuff.
—unidentified Sussex County resident

Ruth and Robert Bosely, young, adventurous newlyweds, wanted a night on the town. She was seventeen, and he was twenty-three, and they lived with Robert's parents in the house next door to the elder Bosely's pharmacy at the corner of Fourteenth and King Streets in Wilmington. Robert was a clerk at his father's store. Ruth lived at 15 East Fourteenth Street, just steps from the Bosely home, and Robert had literally married the girl next door. Ruth and Robert had been married for just over four months, and on Friday night, February 27, 1925, the young couple told Robert's parents that they were going to see a movie.[147]

In 1925, silent movies were in their glory days. The days of the nickelodeon and short films that were an adjunct to vaudeville shows were gone. At the Wilmington movie theaters that dotted Market Street, the Majestic, Queen, Acadia and Rialto, live appearances of performers played second fiddle to the films. When Ruth and Robert went out on Friday night, they had a choice of a variety offerings. *The Speed Spook*, with Johnny Hines, was playing at the Majestic. *Coming Through*, starring Thomas Meighan, paired with the Harry Langdon comedy the *First Hundred Years* was playing at the Queen. The Rialto was screening *The Left-Hand Brand*, with Neal Hart. Most intriguing of all was the Arcadia's *Love's Wilderness*, starring Corinne Griffith. According to the Wilmington *Sunday Morning Star*, she played "a perfect flower of beauty engaged to marry a young scientist of good family....In addition to her excellent work as the young heroine, Miss Griffith further adds to her charm by appearing in numerous new and most attractive gowns." However, When Ruth and Robert said goodbye to his parents, they wanted something more exciting than a movie featuring "new and most attractive gowns."[148]

When they left the Bosely house shortly before 8:00 p.m., they did not head to Market Street, where the major Wilmington movie houses were located; instead, they went a block east to French Street and headed for the Flodette Hotel, where they arrived around 8:15 p.m. and checked into room 232. The next day, the staff at the Flodette Hotel could not remember whether they had left the room after they registered or not. "So many come and go," they said.[149]

The young couple did leave their room that night, and they apparently made the rounds of Wilmington's speakeasies. Before he was married,

Robert liked to go on drinking bouts with his friends. According to his father, "My son is like a lot of the young men about town. He liked to go out at night and drink up some of this liquor that they get nowadays, but I never noticed he was any worse than any of the rest of them." Robert's father also recalled, "I never noticed that Ruth ever took a drink, and I am certain that she never touched drugs. While she was living here in the house with me and Mrs. Bosley and my son, I never noticed that she showed any effect of either liquor or drugs."[150]

The next day, after spending the night drinking with Ruth, Robert, suffering from an acute hangover, was still hazy as to where they specifically went. He remembered taxicab rides and the purchases of liquor in half a dozen places, but he could not recall the exact locations. Bosely was sure that he and his wife had bought two quarts and a pint of liquor and had drunk a most of it. They drank so much that they both passed out in their Flodette Hotel room. At around 5:00 a.m., Robert was awakened by Ruth's groaning. She told Robert that she had agonizing pains in her stomach. Ruth hurt so much that she said she needed a doctor. Robert tried to call a doctor he knew, but the doctor was unavailable. Then Robert, still in the middle of a groggy hangover, passed out.

When Robert woke up, there were several women gathered around his wife. A chambermaid had entered the room around 9:15 a.m. and found the young couple unconscious. The maid called for help, and eventually, a doctor was called. After examining Ruth, the doctor order her to be rushed to the hospital. A police ambulance was summoned, and Ruth was put aboard. Although Robert had regained consciousness, the doctor also ordered him to be taken to the hospital. Ruth died in the ambulance on the way to the hospital.

Except for his horrendous hangover, Robert quickly recovered from his drinking spree. Detained for questioning by the police, he was hazy about where he and Ruth had gone to buy the liquor. "The strange thing," Robert kept repeating, "is how I escaped. I drank ten times as much as my wife did, and I didn't have more than a normal hangover." Finally, he was sent home to get some sleep.[151]

After interviewing Robert and acting on information from other sources, the police immediately conducted a series of raids on suspected speakeasies, including those on Eighth, Robinson and Lincoln Streets. The police made a number of arrests on various alcohol-related charges. The analysis of the liquor that was found in the Bosely's hotel room showed that it contained 35 percent pure grain alcohol, water and artificial coloring matter but no other toxins. It appeared that Ruth had died from simple alcohol poisoning from drinking too much liquor. Since there were no toxins in the alcohol, Robert, an experienced and heavier drinker, could consume the booze without any immediate fatal effects.[152]

The problem of deadly additives to bootleg booze had been a problem from the time Prohibition began. In January 1922, Robert Elliott, the federal director of Prohibition for Delaware, had warned that drinking moonshine was courting a sure death. Bootleggers who were unable to obtain safely distilled grain alcohol were resorting to deadly wood alcohol. Over one hundred deaths attributed to bad whiskey were reported in New York during December 1922, and there were nearly as many alcohol-related deaths in Philadelphia, Chicago and Pittsburgh. Director Elliott said, "Those who are fortunate enough to escape death are slow in recovering. The public should not be unmindful that young girls also crave for the poison whiskey, and only recently, two girls were killed by the stuff. My warning is an appeal for the cooperation of every citizen in Delaware. We must clean our state of the poisoned liquors." Unfortunately, Ruth Bosely did not heed Elliott's warning.[153]

A few months after Ruth's death, the *Wilmington Evening Journal* editorialized:

> *Every Delaware patron of a bootlegger occasionally has a bad moment when he wonders if, by any chance, the stuff he just swallowed put him next on the list of wood alcohol's victims. Millions of people discuss wood alcohol daily. Yet the average person knows next to nothing about this mysterious poison, except that it removes varnish, causes blindness and death, and is used by unscrupulous bootleggers because it is cheap.*[154]

The *Evening Journal* went on to point out:

> *Intoxication from wood alcohol is similar to the effects of pure bonded liquor—at first....A teaspoonful of wood alcohol is sufficient to cause blindness, beginning with double vision, falling of the body's temperature, loss of sensation in the nerve centers, and rhythmic convulsions. A drink of wood alcohol causes blindness 90 times out of 100, and usually means death, though sometimes the patient lingers for as long as a year.*[155]

Several months after the *Evening Journal*'s warning, bootleggers in Sussex County reportedly suffered a slump in sales. According to the *Sunday Morning Star*, "A large number of people, prominent and otherwise, who have been getting their liquor regularly, have sworn off and have stopped drinking. This is not due to any wave of reform which has passed that way but is merely a matter of self protection."[156] Business was so good for one Southern Delaware moonshiner that he could not keep up with the demand. It normally takes about ten days to prepare mash from grain before the mash is distilled. This particular moonshiner discovered that if he treated the grain with an unhealthy dose of lye, the fermentation process was reduced to a matter of hours. When some of his regular customers, however, discovered what he was doing, they declined the lye-laced booze, declaring "Holy horrors! We'll have no more of the stuff.[157]

A few months before Ruth Bosely's death, Oliver Marshall was arrested for violating the liquor laws. Under the guise of medical prescriptions, he was selling additives to give drinks with low alcoholic content a boost. Some of these "prescriptions" were of dubious content and carried names such as "Dragon's Blood" and "Maltazy Fern Tonic." Although some of the ingredients Marshall was pushing were horseradish and other spices, he was nevertheless arrested for violating the liquor laws.[158]

BOMBARDED WITH RIFLE SHOTS

Theodore went out to the car and talked in a friendly manner with him when, suddenly, he struck Clarence in the back with a piece of iron.
—Philadelphia Inquirer

Featuring illegal booze, illicit sex and a simmering family feud, the murder trial of Theodore Lynch attracted so many people that extra state police were called to control the crowds at the Georgetown Courthouse. Lewes, near Cape Henlopen, had been the county seat throughout the colonial period, but after the American Revolution, the growing population of Southern Delaware clamored for a more centrally located county seat. Laid out in 1791, Georgetown in the early twentieth century was usually a quiet town of about 1,500 people—that is, until two days after election day, when the town observed "Return Day."

The tradition of Return Day was born in political strife that dated to the American Revolution. In the late eighteenth century, Delaware elections were held at the county seat, where some voters fought openly in the streets. After the ballot counting was completed, election officials generally waited a day or so to let tempers cool before announcing who had won. When voters returned to Georgetown to hear the election results, the day was dubbed "Return Day," and by 1828, it had become a regular event. Historian J. Thomas Scharf wrote in the late nineteenth century, "One of the customs peculiar to the people of Sussex, from time immemorial, is to hold high carnival on the day when the results of a general election are announced." Scharf went on to explain, "Booths, stalls and stands are erected near the courthouse, where all kinds of edibles, such as opossum and rabbit meat, fish and oysters, can be procured. The women, who constitute a considerable portion of the crowd, are generously treated to cakes, candies, and the best the booths afford."[159]

Although it was not as busy as it was on Return Day, Georgetown became a bustling center of lawyers, lawmakers and others when court was in session. The town also drew crowds from the surrounding area when there was a good execution. In 1813, a detail of troops was dispatched from defending Lewes to Georgetown when there was double hanging of two murderers. The town was also crowded when there was a good trial, such as that of Theodore Lynch.

In December 1925, Prohibition agents had gathered enough evidence to make another sweep through Southern Delaware. The raiding party, composed of state and local police, left Georgetown at 4:00 a.m. on December 12, 1924, and headed for Roxana, where moonshiners had set up a still. The still was reportedly so large that the police had a photographer in tow to record the raid. When the Prohibition agents arrived at Clarence Lynch's house, they did not find any evidence of an illegal still. About one hundred yards behind the house, however, they discovered a twenty-five-gallon still and two barrels of mash. The still was not running at the time, but after searching further, they found ten barrels containing fifty gallons of fermented mash each. The barrels had been partially buried in a trench, and pine slats had been used to camouflage them. It was reputedly the largest bootleg bust in the state.[160]

The Prohibition agents lined up on one side of distilling operation. Albert H. Waller, a prominent photographer from Laurel who had been invited by the Prohibition agents to accompany them on the raid, prepared to take pictures. In the late nineteenth century, the photographer began documenting life in and around Laurel, one of the largest towns in Southern Delaware. Using his Laurel studio as his base, Waller spent a half-century photographing everyday scenes of life in Southern Delaware, and he must have been thrilled to be able to photograph an actual raid

The large bootleg still near Roxana was photographed by Albert H. Waller of Laurel, who accompanied the Prohibition agents. *Courtesy of the Delaware Public Archives.*

on a moonshiner's still.[161] Moments after Waller had snapped the first photographs of the raiding party standing by half-buried barrels of mash, his picture-taking was interrupted by the sharp, crackling sound of gunfire. According to the *State Register*, "The officers were bombarded with rifle shots."[162]

The agents returned fire, but they were in the open, and their assailants were hidden in the woods. The firing was so intense that several tree limbs were shot off and fell amid the still, the barrels of mash and the retreating lawmen. Unlike other raids, the ambush did not lead to a protracted gun battle. When the agents realized that they could not see the moonshiners, the lawmen decided to abandon the still. After briefly considering that the moonshiners might ambush them as the agents made their way out of the woods, they left the still and reached their cars without incident. The Prohibition agents had shut down the largest still in Southern Delaware, and Waller had taken some great photographs, but the consequences of the raid were definitely not over.[163]

The Lynch family of fourteen siblings was large, but it was not happy. There was bad blood between older brother Theodore, aged forty-five, and younger brother Clarence, thirty-two, because, as the *State Register* put it, "the alleged infidelity of his Theodore's wife and her apparent intimacy with Clarence."[164] A week after the raid on the Lynch farm, Theodore, his wife, Mary Lynch, and a friend, Marion Mills, went to Clarence's house, ostensibly to butcher some hogs that the brothers owned together. When they arrived, however, Theodore pulled out a revolver and declared that he would kill his brother. Fortunately, the women got the gun away from him and hid it in a corn stack, and the frustrated Theodore returned home.

A few hours later, Clarence apparently decided to see if Theodore's temper had subsided, and it was dark when Clarence drove over to his brother's farm. According to the *Philadelphia Inquirer*:

> *Theodore went out to the car and talked in a friendly manner with him when, suddenly, he struck Clarence in the back with a piece of iron. While he pleaded to be spared...the older brother pulled Clarence from the*

This Waller photograph of the Roxana still with the Prohibition agents was taken moments before the bootleggers opened fire. *Courtesy of the Delaware Public Archives.*

automobile and, with his butcher knife, cut his throat and threw him on the ground. He then ran up and kicked his wife off the step. She threw a lighted lantern at him, and the two women ran and hid in the corn field.[165]

While his brother was dying on the ground, Theodore got into his car and drove off, shouting that he would come back later and kill them all. After Theodore left, his wife and her friend emerged from the cornfield, wrapped Clarence's corpse in a blanket and carried it inside the house. The authorities learned of the altercation, and when a detective arrived to investigate, he found the lifeless body in the kitchen on a couch.

At first, it was thought that Theodore had fled into the swamps, but his car was found stuck in a ditch by the side of the road in Selbyville, on the border of Maryland. This led them to believe that he had left Delaware, but that was not the case. He was soon apprehended and charged with murder.[166] His trial in Georgetown attracted so much attention that extra state police were on duty to handle the crowd, which filled the courtroom to overflowing. At Theodore's trial, his wife testified that her husband was jealous of the attention that Clarence was giving her. She also testified that Theodore had threatened to kill Clarence several times. On the other hand, Roxie Lynch, the widow of the murdered Clarence, testified in favor of her brother-in-law, Theodore. When Theodore, who the *Philadelphia Inquirer* reported was "more or less insane since an attack of the influenza some years ago," testified in his own behalf, he admitted to the details of the slaying.[167] But he contended that he "was not the aggressor in the fight."[168] Theodore said he was enraged by the affair that Clarence was having with wife. At 5:00 p.m. on Tuesday, the case was given to the jury, who deliberated for fifteen hours and found Theodore guilty of second-degree murder. He was sentenced to life imprisonment.

Shootout in Wilmington

I have something important to tell him.
—*Thomas E. Blakeley, Wilmington police officer*

The gunfight was reminiscent of the classic Western standoffs in unruly nineteenth-century frontier towns like Deadwood, Dodge City or at the O.K. Corral in Tombstone. Late at night on June 29, 1924, suspected bootlegger

Alducci (Tedaldo) Di Sabatino, along with three of his cohorts, pulled up in a car near his home on narrow Third Street, between Lincoln and Union Streets on the border of Wilmington's Little Italy neighborhood. Two other cars with several federal Prohibition agents and an informer were parked nearby. Agents Ira Melvin, Lee Washburn, Albert Dillahay and Joseph Hermann got out their cars and approached Sabatino as he was preparing to open the gate that led to his parking spot. Agent Melvin said something to Sabatino, and immediately, the men on the street pulled out their guns and opened fire. Melvin dropped to the ground, and a bullet from Sabatino's gun passed over him and hit agent Dillahay in the neck. Agents Washburn and Herman had a clear field of fire and shot Sabatino several times. The suspected bootlegger died on the Third Street sidewalk.

The gunfight was over so quickly that the men who had accompanied Sabatino were not able to get out of the car and take part in it. None of the dead man's cohorts were arrested, and after the shooting, some of his friends said he often had large amounts of cash with him and that he was afraid that the federal agents were thieves who were attempting to rob him, so he fired in self-defense. On three separate occasions, evidence was presented to a grand jury against the agents, but they refused to indict them.[169]

Almost two years later, Edwin C. Totten from Laurel, Delaware, wrote a multipart series of articles on his experiences as a federal Prohibition agent with the ponderous title "Truth from the Inside about Delaware Prohibition Enforcement." Totten commented on the Sabatino shooting in a segment headlined "The Wilmington Killing And Public Sentiment." While Totten was not one of the four agents who was connected with the fatal shooting of Sabatino, he wrote, "There has never been [an] occurrence in the criminal history [of] the state, which a greater wave of [indignation] was expressed publicly."[170]

Totten, as a former enforcement agent, was generally supportive of the police, but two weeks after the suspected bootlegger Sabatino was gunned down on the streets of Wilmington, a bust on a major speakeasy uncovered the sales on illegal hooch and much more. On Wednesday, July 8, 1925, Prohibition agents seeking evidence of illegal booze raided what was popularly called the "Lawless Hotel." Although the name was certainly appropriate for the establishment, which the *Sunday Morning Star* described as "a free-and-easy booze-gambling-bawdy-house," the name came from the original owner, Thomas Lawless.[171] Located on the northern edge of the city at the intersection of Barley Mill and Montchanin Roads, the Lawless Hotel had a reputation for serving illegal booze, loose women and high-stakes gambling tables. During the raid, Prohibition agents found all three. One of the men arrested was William Paulman, who was charged with operating a gambling table. Paulman was fined $1,000, which he paid, according to the *Sunday Morning Star*, "in United States currency of different dominations, some $100 bills, some $50 and some as low as $1 and $2."[172] The nabbing of William Paulman led to the arrest of his brother James, who was described by the *Sunday Morning Star* as "dashing and debonair, driving around most of his leisure time in a Chrysler car, licensed 6,642, but made himself a figure for police and bootleggers to conjure with."[173] Jimmy Paulman, a member of the Wilmington police force, was friendly with the then-present owners of the Lawless Hotel, and after the raid on the hotel, he turned in his badge. With his usual bravado, after he resigned from the police force, he drove out of the courtyard in the rear of the police station, waving goodbye to his friends. A short time later, he was arrested for possessing bootleg liquor in his car and in his house.

Jimmy Paulman was not the only police officer who was implicated in the Lawless Hotel scandal. Police sergeant William Vandegrift also resigned immediately after the raid and announced that he was going back to his old job as a bricklayer, which raised eyebrows because the bricklaying business was not rushed for work.[174] A short time later, Vandegrift was arrested for accepting a bribe of $200 from a man who wanted to fix two liquor charges against him.[175] Both Paulman and Vandegrift were allowed to resign without giving the usual ten days' notice, which would have permitted these two men to return to the force at some future time. After a public uproar and following an investigation, the directors of the police force rescinded their actions and summoned the two disgraced officers for a hearing. Paulman and Vandegrift declined to attend the hearing, and the two officers were dismissed outright.[176]

The Sabatino case and the raid on the Lawless Hotel generated a great deal of speculation about corruption in the law enforcement establishment, and in the case of the Wilmington Police Department, it sensationally affected Superintendent Black.

On Saturday, October 17, 1925, at around 10:00 p.m., the phone rang at Black's home at Delaware Avenue and Lincoln Street. George A. Black, a Wilmington policeman and the son of Superintendent Black, picked up the phone, and the person on the other end of the line refused to give his name and. The caller asked, "Is the chief home yet?" George Black answered, "No." The caller then asked, "Well, I have something important to tell him. When will he be home?" George Black told the man that his father would probably be home no later than 11:00 p.m., and the stranger told George to tell his father when he got home that he would meet him on the front lawn, repeating that he had something important to tell him.

When Superintendent Black returned home shortly before 11:00 p.m., his son told him of the strange call. Looking out the window, the superintendent and his son could see a man walking along Delaware Avenue. "That looks like Tom Blakeley," remarked the superintendent, "he must have been drinking something." Officer Thomas E. Blakeley had recently been suspended from the Wilmington Police Force for raping a nineteen-year-old girl at his home. The superintendent then walked out to the entrance of his yard and met Blakeley. His son remained on the porch. After a few words with Blakeley, Superintendent Black exclaimed, "Well, anybody that told you that lied. You had better go home." He then placed his hand on Blakeley's arm in an attempt to manhandle him on his way. Blakely took a step back, pulled a revolver from his pocket and fired at Black twice in quick succession. One bullet struck Black in his right side, under his arm, and was deflected by a rib, passing across the chest under the skin. The second bullet hit the superintendent in the left forearm.

The two shots staggered Black back a step. After regaining his balance, Black lunged forward and grabbed Blakeley. The superintendent attempted to wrest the pistol from Blakeley's hand, and the disgraced officer continued to hold tight to the revolver as the two men fell to the ground. As the two men wrestled, the weapon was fired a third time, and the bullet hit Blakeley's head. While the former officer lay on the ground, Black got up and was met by his son, who had drawn his revolver. The younger Black was attempting to shoot Blakeley when his father snatched the gun from him. He told his son to keep calm and to not do anything he would regret.

George took Bleckley's revolver and the weapon he had drawn from his own holster and took them into to the house. He then rushed to the garage in the rear of the building to get his father's car. By the time George had driven to the front of the house, a crowd had gathered, and some of the bystanders helped get the superintendent into the car. George then drove his father to the hospital. In the meantime, the police ambulance was called, and Blakeley was also taken to the hospital. Both men eventually recovered from their wounds, and Blakely was sentenced to six years in prison for shooting Superintendent Black. Commenting on the shooting of the former police officer and the superintendent, the *Wilmington Sunday Morning Star* editorialized:

The double shooting marked the high sport of a series of charges and countercharges, attacks and counterattacks, resignations and dismissals that have marred the record of the local police department for some time. Each week has brought its new sensation, and it has been a poor period that did not show someone on trial before the safety department. It is generally believed that the end is not yet and that, out of the seething ferment in the department, sensational disclosures are yet to come.[177]

Former agent Edwin Totten, who defended the agents in the Alducci Sabatino shooting, wrote in March 1926, "At various times, I had beard reports and talk relative to protection being given the violator, especially in Wilmington, but I had paid but little attention to it, classing it mostly as idle gossip." During the previous year, the idle gossip had reached a crescendo in the aftermath of the killing of Sabatino, the raid on the Lawless Hotel and the incident at Superintendent Black's house. Wilmington residents and others began to think that corruption in the Wilmington Police Department was not just frivolous talk.

Totten uncovered several incriminating facts, but he was not able to tie everything together. Just before he resigned as a Prohibition agent, he learned that corruption in the Wilmington police force was being looked at by another agency. Totten wrote in the *Sunday Morning Star* (Totten's original italicization and capitulations have been retained):

> *There has been an insistent report regarding two "lists," which were said to be operated in Wilmington on the following basis:*
>
> *A certain class of violators are reported to have paid TEN DOLLARS EACH WEEK FOR PROTECTION while another class paid fifteen. This was supposed to insure their protection, but if apprehended, they were to have no redress other than to have a bondsman provided...*I learned that this protection ring included a prominent saloon-keeper who had himself never been apprehended, *although alleged to be operating widely,* and several other men *who were rated high in their respective lines.*[178]

THE TRUTH ABOUT PROHIBITION

DELAWARE LAUNCHES A COUNTERATTACK

Tomorrow morning, with no more ceremony than the post of a notice, one of the most important public works ever undertaken in the state of Delaware will have reached its practical conclusion.
—Sunday Morning Star

During the first few years of Prohibition, rumrunning motherships, hovering just beyond the three-mile limit, openly unloaded their illegal booze onto a flotilla of small boats that slipped ashore. As time went on, the impromptu bootleggers were replaced with better-organized gangsters, and an estimated one hundred thousand cases of illegal hooch were smuggled ashore each month along the Atlantic Coast.[179] A case of whiskey distilled legally in a foreign country cost a bootlegger about $15 and was often sold in the United States for more than twice that price. A single rumrunning schooner, like the one sighted off Rehoboth Beach, could carry more than $1 million worth of booze.[180] The Coast Guard was clearly overmatched in its efforts to stem this flood of booze.

The U.S. Coast Guard was formed in 1915 by combining the revenue service, which was charged with intercepting smugglers, and the life-saving service, which maintained a series of stations along the coast to assist mariners in distress. The Coast Guard took over the existing life-saving stations in Delaware at Lewes, Cape Henlopen, Rehoboth, Indian River Inlet, Bethany Beach and Fenwick Island. Although the crews of these stations were on the lookout for rumrunners landing their illicit cargo, the Coast Guard did not have enough vessels to maintain its normal duties while patrolling the coast for potential rumrunners.[181] The Coast Guard estimated that it seized a woeful 5 percent of the illegal hooch that was flowing into the United States from the sea. In 1924, a $13.8 million plan to augment the Coast Guard's fleet was approved to recondition twenty-two old vessels that had been transferred from the navy and to construct 323 smaller patrol vessels.[182]

The Vinyard Shipyard in Milford secured a contract to build ten of the fast-running seventy-five-foot-long Coast Guard patrol boats.[183] Founded by Wilson Vinyard in 1896 on the south bank of the Mispillion River, the Vinyard Shipyard was one of seven shipyards in Milford at the end of the nineteenth century, when the shipbuilding industry in many Delaware River towns was at its peak. At that time, many of these shipyards were building some of the last of the commercial sailing schooners. During World I, however, the Vinyard Shipyard built subchasers for the United States Navy,

The Vinyard Shipyard in Milford built ten fast-running vessels for the Coast Guard, including *CG-218. Courtesy of the Delaware Public Archives.*

and it was already experienced in constructing fast, powerful cruisers when it received the contract for the Coast Guard patrol boats. During the later years of Prohibition, the shipyard also built stylish luxury power yachts.[184] The patrol boats built at Vinyard were assigned to Coast Guard installations along the East Coast. *CG-218* was stationed at Prohibition Patrol Base No. 9 at Cape May and helped suppress the rumrunners that were operating near the mouth of Delaware Bay.[185] The repairation of the old navy ships and the construction of new patrol boats took some time, as did the recruitment and training of the five thousand officers and men who crewed these additional Coast Guard vessels.[186]

In addition to modernizing the Coast Guard, in 1924, the United States negotiated treaties with several European countries to extend the territorial waters of the United States to "an hour's steaming distance"—generally, twelve miles.[187] With motherships standing farther away from the coast, the small boats that ferried booze to shore had a longer run and a greater chance of being spotted by the Coast Guard. The rumrunners adopted a clever tactic to thwart being captured. The slowest of the boats was designated as a decoy. After the small rumrunners were loaded, they would head for shore. If they were spotted by the authorities, the decoy would lag behind the others and be overtaken by the Coast Guard. While the Coast Guard personnel were busy detaining and searching the decoy, the other rumrunners escaped with their cargoes.[188] The bootleggers also developed low-draft speedboats with closed pillbox pilot houses. With armor-plated sides and powered by as many as four engines, some of these rumrunners could carry as much as one thousand cases of hooch and speed to shore at thirty-two knots.[189]

In October 1925, the federal authorities made a concerted effort to clean up Delaware and the Eastern Shore of Maryland and rid them of bootleggers and rumrunners. They estimated that if they could shut down twenty stills in that area, the illegal alcohol business would be crippled. The problem with the suppression of illegal booze was that it would take an army of agents to ensure that the country was dry. Once a still was raided, another opened up to take its place. Bootlegging, the federal officials maintained, was like "malignant cancer—cut it out at one place, and it breaks out at another."[190]

A month after the federal authorities began their efforts to cleanse Delaware and the Eastern Shore of Maryland of bootleggers, the last load of concrete was poured on the Du Pont Boulevard. This road would have a great effect on rumrunners and enforcement agents. The Du Pont Boulevard

Opposite, top: The Vinyard Shipyard gained experience by constructing small vessels for the military during World War I. *Courtesy of the Delaware Public Archives.*

Opposite, bottom: During Prohibition, the Vinyard Shipyard also built fast-running pleasure boats, such as the *Navigo*, seen here passing the Lightship Overfalls off Cape Henlopen. *Courtesy of the Delaware Public Archives.*

Right: T. Coleman du Pont financed the construction of the Du Pont Boulevard, which reached from one end of Delaware to the other. *Courtesy of the Library of Congress.*

was the brainchild of T. Coleman du Pont. In the early twentieth century, many of the roads of rural Delaware originated as narrow forest paths the Natives established long before the first European colonists arrived. As the European settlements grew, the colonists widened the trails, but throughout the nineteenth century, most of Delaware's roads remained unpaved. In wet weather, the state's "highways" became muddy quagmires that made land travel nearly impossible.

By the beginning of the twentieth century, however, the first horseless carriages began bouncing along the bone-jarring roads. By 1910, cars were becoming commonplace, but the poor condition of Delaware's roads made driving long distances a daunting task. Delaware had no statewide highway department to oversee the construction of a modern road system when T. Coleman du Pont announced his extraordinary plan to build a divided, paved highway from one end of Delaware to the other. He also announced that he would present it as his gift to the state. After assembling a team of highway engineers, du Pont bought land for the right-of-way, gathered a fleet of road-building equipment and hired construction crews. A year after he made the proposal, du Pont and his squad of experts were motoring over the rutted roads of Southern Delaware, scouting routes for the new highway. The initial section of the road was constructed at the state line near Selbyville, but work was slowed by World War I. After the war, work was resumed, and on November 18, 1923, the *Wilmington Sunday Morning Star* announced, "Tomorrow morning, with no more ceremony than the post of a notice, one of the most important public works ever undertaken in the state of Delaware will have reached its practical conclusion. The last concrete has been poured on the Du Pont Boulevard."[191]

The opening of the last link north of Dover completed ninety miles of continuous paved highway from the south side of Wilmington to Selbyville at the Delaware–Maryland border. Soon, vehicles loaded with produce from Delaware farms, cars driven by people who were out for a pleasant Sunday drive and trucks hauling bootleg whiskey began traveling the Du Pont Boulevard.

A week before Christmas in 1925, six empty trucks started from Philadelphia, and when they reached the southern edge of Wilmington, they began to drive on the northern leg of the Du Pont Boulevard (Route 13). Just south of Dover, Route 13 intersected Route 113, which formed

Because his new highway cut through undeveloped sections of Delaware, du Pont used a car outfitted with tents as his home when he supervised the construction of the new road. *Courtesy of the Library of Congress.*

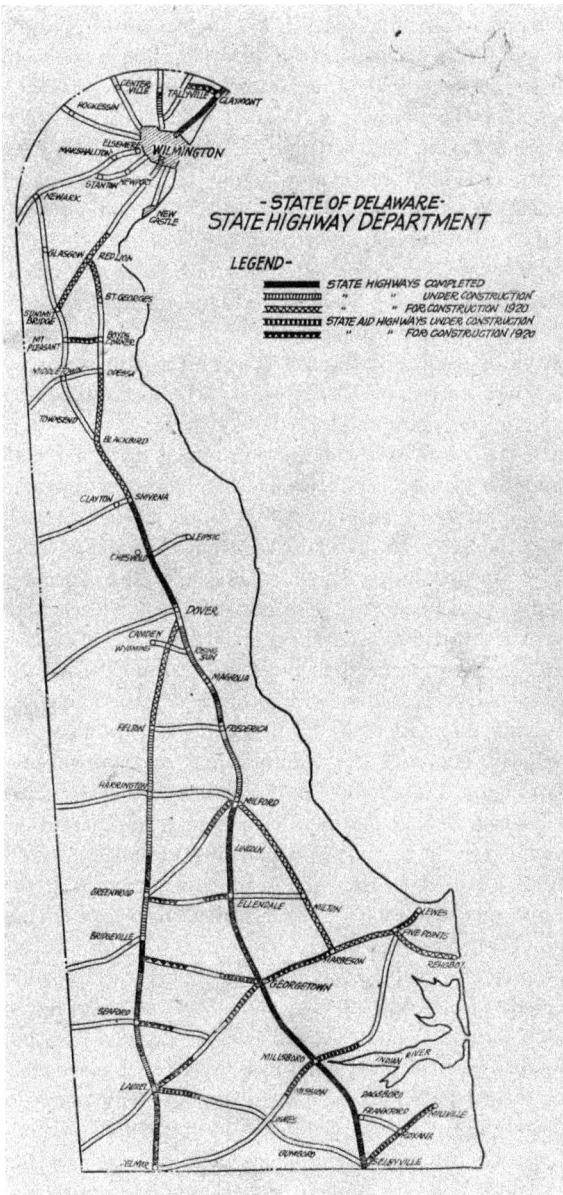

The construction
of new roads
during Prohibition
opened up sections
of Southern
Delaware to
bootleggers.
*Courtesy of the
Delaware Public
Archives.*

the southern leg of the Du Pont Boulevard. It is not clear what route the bootleggers followed, but the southern part of the Du Pont Boulevard, from Dover to Selbyville, near the Maryland border, was a consistently better road than Route 13, which ended farther west at Delmar, on the border between Delaware and Maryland. Taking the Du Pont Boulevard would also have put the convoy of trucks closer to Ocean City when the bootleggers crossed into Maryland. After the trucks entered Maryland, where the roads were not as good, they made their way to Berlin and turned eastward toward Ocean City. Riding over the new drawbridge and into town, the bootleggers' trucks pulled up to a deserted spot on the beach. At that time, Ocean City only extended to around Sixteenth Street, and there was no inlet that separated the Maryland resort from Assateague Island. There were also no paved roads along the coast that connected Ocean City with Fenwick Island and the other Delaware oceanfront communities.

When the drivers of the convoy met with the rumrunners on Ocean City Beach, they discovered that a small fleet of twenty fast motorboats were able to slip past the Coast Guard vessels and successfully land a horde of hooch on the beach. Like the other resort towns on the Delaware–Maryland Coast, Ocean City was nearly deserted during the wintertime, and the bootleggers had little to fear from the local residents. The rumrunners, however, were alarmed at the news that a squad of federal agents had learned about the operation and were enroute to Ocean City. Both the rumrunners and the law enforcement agents had their sources within the other's operations. As a snitch alerted the agents that a big delivery of booze was to be made on the Ocean City beach, an informer of the rumrunners said that twenty-two agents from Washington, D.C., had been dispatched to the Maryland resort to intercept the illegal alcohol. At that time, crossing the Chesapeake Bay required a lengthy ride on a ferry, and reaching Ocean City from Washington, D.C., took a half day or more. On the other hand, a simple phone call from the informer to Salisbury enabled a messenger to reach the bootleggers in Ocean City in plenty of time.

Knowing that the agents were on their way, the rumrunners quickly loaded their trucks and headed out of town. The drivers believed that the agents might pursue them on the Du Pont Boulevard, so they decided to swing westward and use the backroads of Maryland's Eastern Shore to make their way north until they turned to the east and went through Wilmington to safely deliver their illegal cargo, valued at $200,000, to Philadelphia.[192]

Although the Coast Guard had begun a counterattack against the rumrunners, the Du Pont Boulevard brought more landing places on the coast within the reach of the landing boats. When a hard-surfaced road was connecting the Lewes and Rehoboth areas, the number of landing places increased for the bootleggers. In addition to the cooperation of local residents, the bootleggers were better organized. They knew the back roads, they had informers and they devised codes and other strategies to prevent capture. On the other hand, the law enforcement officers were divided by federal, state and local departments, and they sometimes lacked good coordination, which allowed the bootleggers to slip away.

Dapper Dan Collins

Detectives? Why, they couldn't detect a horseshoe in a plate of hash.
—Dapper Dan Collins, bootlegger

Edwin Totten wrote in the fourth installment of his newspaper series describing his experiences as a Prohibition agent, "We had complaint from Wilmington and also Philadelphia that the notorious 'Dapper Dan' Collins was in or about Delaware City, plying his alleged trade of rum smuggling from the Bahamas."[193] Dapper Dan, whose real name was Robert A. Tourbillion, was one of the more colorful characters that Prohibition produced. Born in the 1880s, probably near Atlanta, Georgia, his first job was in a circus act, where he rode a bicycle in a cage full of lions.[194] The swaggering bravado that Collins demonstrated in a cage full of real lions served him well when he graduated to a career of stealing, swindling and bootlegging. Tall, suave and impeccably groomed, Collins could have served as a model for Jay Gatsby in F. Scott's Fitzgerald's 1925 novel *The Great Gatsby*.[195] Collins was in and out of prison on several occasions, and at one of his several trials, he was asked by the prosecutor, "Why do you have so many names and aliases on the police records?" Collins replied, "Oh, the coppers call me anything." The prosecutor continued, "By coppers, I presume you mean detectives?" Dapper Dan smoothly shot back, "Detectives? Why, they couldn't detect a horseshoe in a plate of hash."[196]

The handsome bootlegger was familiar with the Delaware Bay, which he reportedly sailed often on the way to Philadelphia, once on a rumrunner that was filled with booze and sometimes crewed by five attractive women. Prohibition agent Totten's encounter with Collins began when several men who identified themselves as government agents stopped at Totten's

Dapper Dan Collins reportedly sailed a rumrunner on the Delaware Bay with an all-female crew. Evening Journal, *February 6, 1922.*

house and asked his wife where he was. Mrs. Totten warily asked for identification, and when they failed to produce any credentials, the supposed agents left. Shortly afterward, Mrs. Totten told her husband of the incident, and he traced one of these bogus agents to Delaware City, about a dozen miles south of Wilmington, and he immediately set off in pursuit.[197]

In the early 1920s, Delaware City was a busy small town of about one thousand residents, sitting at the eastern end of the Chesapeake and Delaware Canal, where it emptied into the Delaware Bay. Late in the afternoon on February 1, 1922, Totten boarded a trolley for Delaware City, but a heavy snowstorm stalled the trolley at Red Lion, about four miles from Totten's destination. With the other passengers, the Prohibition agent abandoned the trolley and began to trudge through the deep snow to Delaware City. Tired, wet and hungry, Totten set about trying to locate the man who had posed as a Prohibition agent. At a poolroom, he engaged in casual conversation with one of the patrons, who let drop the startling news that Dapper Dan Collins was in town. Totten was skeptical at first, but the man in the poolroom claimed that he had met Collins on previous visits to Delaware City. Totten, always on the lookout for capturing, as he called Collins, a "big operator," carried a small photograph and a written description of the famous bootlegger. The poolroom informant told Totten that Collins was at a small restaurant in town, and the agent immediately set out in pursuit. According to Totten, "I was well aware that Collins was believed by the authorities, who wanted him on several charges, to be a dangerous man. He was said to carry two guns in shoulder holsters and was decidedly quick on the draw." Totten was not deterred by Dapper Dan's reputation, and the agent prepared for a shootout. As Totten recalled, "With these thoughts in mind, I changed my gun—I discarded the little .32 and wore a .38 special—from a shoulder holster to my outside overcoat pocket. I planned to corner Collins on sight and put him under arrest."[198]

Totten went to the restaurant where the poolhall informer believed Dapper Dan was dining, but when looking through a door window, Totten could see no one resembling the infamous bootlegger. Disappointed and still hungry, Totten entered the eatery, placed his overcoat on a hook near the stove and took a seat at a table some distance away. After ordering ham, eggs and coffee, he began reading a newspaper while waiting for his food. Totten recalled, "I read a brief article or two and on looking up was practically stunned when I saw the man I believed to be 'Dapper Dan' seated at an adjoining table—and directly between me and my overcoat. I had left my gun in my overcoat pocket."[199]

The Prohibition agent was stunned. He was sure the man at the next table was Dapper Dan Collins, but Totten was powerless without his weapon. Totten pondered his next move, and he later recalled, "It was a rather critical few minutes for me…but it was probably fortunate that circumstances prevented immediate action." After gulping down the coffee and tasteless ham and eggs, Totten was about to get up and retrieve his overcoat with his pistol when the waiter asked if the agent was going to Wilmington. Totten said that he would like to, and the stranger Totten believed to be Collins spoke up and said he was going that way and that Totten could ride in his truck. Totten jumped at the opportunity to get the stranger alone, figuring his chances of capturing him in Wilmington were better than in Delaware City, where the supposed criminal might have had friends lurking about.[200]

The trip to Wilmington was uneventful, aside from the fact that the man Totten intended to arrest was silent much of the time. The stranger carried two large suitcases, which Totten believed contained drugs or liquor, and his plan was to arrest him when they arrived at Wilmington. During the truck ride, one of the few things the stranger did say was that he was a novelty salesman and that the suitcases contained his wares. Crestfallen, the Prohibition agent concluded the man was not the "Dapper Dan" Collins of bootlegging fame. Totten later wrote, "I have seen him several times since but never informed him of the error I might have made.…I quite modestly refrained from entering this 'near arrest' in my official reports. I was under the impression it might be looked upon as the result of drinking too much 'near beer.'"[201]

Robert A. Tourbillion continued his nefarious ways, but after Prohibition ended, he fell on hard times. In 1939, he was convicted of stealing $200 from an immigrant in an immigration racket and was sentenced to fifteen to twenty years in Sing Sing. In November 1949, eight months after the old bootlegger was transferred to Attica, he died of heart disease.[202]

Rumrunners Lose a Landmark

I doubt sincerely if one man could have secured enough evidence to ever apprehend a boat single-handed in this section.
—Edwin C. Totten, federal Prohibition agent

At the start of Prohibition, the Delaware Coast was bracketed by two lighthouses, Cape Henlopen Lighthouse at the northern end of the coast, and Fenwick Island Lighthouse to the south. The Cape Henlopen Lighthouse was built a decade before the American Revolution, and it maintained watch over the shifting sands that were eroding the dunes at its base. The Fenwick Island Lighthouse was built in the middle of the nineteenth century, and it stood just a few yards from Delaware's border with Maryland. Built to guide legitimate mariners past the dangerous coastal waters, in the 1920s, the two Delaware lighthouses steered illegal rumrunners to safe places where they could land their hooch.

On the bayside of Cape Henlopen and within sight of the lighthouse, Lewes was the granddaddy of Delaware coastal communities. Founded in the seventeenth century, Lewes was the saltiest town in the First State. It was steeped in tradition and dominated by the smelly fishing processing plants on the bay shore, near the town's bathing beach. When debris from the processing plants drifted over to the bathers at Lewes Beach, they calmly brushed them out of the way and continued playing in the water. Many residents of Lewes, a large number of whom were watermen, were opposed to Prohibition, and illegal booze was sold from the trunks of cars parked near Lewes Beach.

For two centuries, Lewes was the only substantial community on the Delaware Coast, but in 1873, a new neighbor, Rehoboth Beach, was established about a half dozen miles south of Lewes on the ocean coast. Rehoboth was founded by a church group that did not allow alcohol, gambling or dancing, but as the resort grew, it discarded its religious underpinnings, and liquor flowed freely. After the Du Pont Boulevard was completed, a hard-surfaced road was built to link Lewes and Rehoboth to the new highway, allowing vacationers and bootleggers easy access to both towns. Once a seaside resort for the residents of Southern Delaware, vacationers from Wilmington, Baltimore and, particularly, Washington, D.C., were then flooding into Rehoboth, where they bought new vacation homes in Rehoboth Heights and Henlopen Acres.

Dewey Beach, just south of Rehoboth, was founded by oceangoers who could not accept Rehoboth's early religious strictures, and during

The Fenwick Island Lighthouse at Delaware's southern border stood watch over a desolate part of the coast. *Photographn by Michael Morgan.*

Taken from the top of the Fenwick Island Lighthouse, this photograph shows how undeveloped the Delaware Coast was during Prohibition. *Courtesy of the Delaware Public Archives.*

Cars on Lewes Beach sold hooch from their trunks. *Courtesy of the Delaware Public Archives.*

Prohibition, it was a straggling collection of beach cottages and freewheeling establishments that developed around the former Rehoboth Beach Life-Saving Station. Delaware's newest ocean resort during Prohibition was Bethany Beach, located several miles south of Dewey Beach. Many of the young resort's two hundred permanent residents lived in large, comfortable beach houses. Boasting a modest, short boardwalk that was shorter and quieter than Rehoboth's, Bethany was a resort where visitors went to meet friends, talk and eat ice cream. Six miles south of Bethany stood the Fenwick Island Lighthouse and a collection of small beach cottages.

Delaware's oceanfront communities were separated by the natural dunes of state-owned lands and the coastal bays that ran parallel to the sandy strip of land that held the beach towns. Bethany Beach was anchored firmly to the mainland by a wide neck of land that held dirt roads that ran through several Southern Delaware towns until they reached the Du Pont Boulevard. Fenwick Island was also linked to the mainland by a bridge over a narrow, manmade channel of water that was affectionately known as the "Ditch," which separated Fenwick from the rest of Delaware. Although the Coast Guard had taken over the former life-saving stations at Rehoboth Beach, Indian River Inlet, Bethany Beach and Fenwick Island, the isolation of the Delaware beach communities made them ideal landing spots for rumrunners. In particular, the Lewes and Rehoboth area, with its concrete road connections to the Du Pont Boulevard, was favored by bootleggers who were concocting moonshine on land and rumrunners who were bringing hooch ashore.

In 1922, when the two "Gentlemen Moonshiners," Dan Schimer and Jack Wolf, were apprehended near Rehoboth, Prohibition agents believed that they had put a serious dent in the supply of illegal alcohol in Southern Delaware, but the distilling of illicit hooch continued. On November 29, 1924, agents raided three Sussex County farms and found illegal stills. One operation near Millsboro on the western side of the coastal bays had three thirty-gallon stills. Another raid near the Maryland border netted a forty-gallon and a twenty-gallon still, and at the third raid north of Georgetown, agents found three twenty-gallon stills.[203] Several months later, in April 1925, the federal Prohibition detective for Delaware Robert B. Elliott resigned and was replaced by William J. Swain of Bridgeville. Swain was a well-known politician, former state treasurer and insurance commissioner.[204] Swain immediately began a sweep of suspected bootleggers in Southern Delaware.[205] When a Prohibition agent noticed a flock of birds feeding in a ditch in a swamp near Georgetown, he went to investigate and discovered that the birds were eating mash residue that had overflowed into a stream leading to the ditch. Calling the state highway police for assistance, the officers followed the stream for a mile and a half until they located a still that was running at full blast, and they arrested the two moonshiners. On the same day, Prohibition agents raided a crowded speakeasy in Laurel. When the agents went in through the front door, the patrons flooded out through a back door, leaving only two men behind. One man was unconscious and the other was "in a stupefied condition."[206] Two weeks later, agents arrested sixty-eight-year-old Charles B. Marvil for serving literal bootleg liquor. When agents went to his home near Selbyville in Southern Delaware and bought liquor, Marvil dipped the booze from an old rubber boot and gave it to them.[207] Needless to say, Marvil was arrested for selling illegal liquor.

Before he retired, Prohibition agent Edwin Totten was in charge of the coastal area, and in his newspaper series about illegal booze and the problems of Prohibition enforcement, he commented, "A large number of complaints were coming from Rehoboth and Lewes at this time, as the summer rush was on there."[208] Totten spent considerable time investigating both towns, and he discovered that the residents of Lewes and Rehoboth were sympathetic to the bootleggers, and they were indisposed to give any significant information about the rumrunners and their activities. Lewes resident Elizabeth (Lizzie) Carter commented in her diary, "Heard that two or three women from town and a man who lives not far from us have been arrested for bootlegging. Lewes is certainly getting notorious."[209]

As this young lady demonstrates, illegal booze was often transported to Rehoboth in small containers that visitors carried with them to the resort. *Courtesy of the Library of Congress.*

Totten wrote, "During those investigations, I found, especially at Rehoboth, that much of the liquor reported to be so plentiful was being supplied by the 'hip pocket' route. By this, I mean that a large portion of it was brought to our coast resort by private individuals, and the drinking was from the private flask to a large extent."[210] Although Totten spotted a number of intoxicated people at the resort, he believed that there was no practical way of stopping Rehoboth visitors from bringing their booze from home. This was also the case at Oak Orchard on the west side of the coastal bay, near Millsboro.

In addition to people bringing hooch from home when they visited the coastal communities, Totten was troubled by numerous reports of boats landing liquor near Lewes. Several people came up to him with empty scotch bottles with their original labels and asked why Totten did not apprehend the bootleggers who were landing the booze. The Prohibition agent complained, "I was working almost entirely alone, and with more complaints than one man could handle, it would have been impossible to drop all else and take a chance on picking up a boat landing liquor along the Lewes shoreline, when these landings were irregular, infrequent and made with much care."[211] He said that his superiors would have complained if he spent all of his time lounging around Lewes on the off chance that he would catch a rumrunner in the act of landing illicit cargo. Totten lamented, "I doubt sincerely if one man could have secured enough evidence to ever apprehend a boat single-handed in this section."[212]

When a mothership loaded with booze anchored outside of the newly established twelve-mile limit, the rumrunners loaded smaller, speedier boats for the run to the shore. The old Cape Henlopen Lighthouse was the tallest structure on the beach, and it provided a convenient landmark to guide the bootleggers around the cape to bayside landing points near Lewes. In 1926, however, it was no secret that the Cape Henlopen Lighthouse was in trouble. When the beacon was constructed in 1765, the builders placed the lighthouse near the end of a ridge of sand that ran across the northern face of Cape Henlopen. At that time, the lighthouse stood a quarter mile from the surf, amid trees and shrubs that covered the top of the dune. Within a few decades of its construction, it became evident that the dune on which the lighthouse stood was slowly eroding away. The prevalent onshore winds carried the sand from the face of the dune, up and over its top, killing the trees and shrubs whose roots once held the sand in place. In some years, the dunes migrated westward by an estimated thirty to fifty feet. By the beginning of Prohibition, the moving sand left the old lighthouse on the edge of a sandy precipice, with parts of the foundation of the tower exposed.

Debris from the keeper's house litters the dune, foreshadowing the demise of the lighthouse. *Courtesy of the Delaware Public Archives.*

Throughout the nineteenth and early twentieth centuries, the lighthouse was considered an important aid to navigation, and there were several attempts to stop the erosion that threatened it. Wooden groins were constructed to stem the flow of sand away from the dune's base, but they were too little, too late. When the passenger liner *Lenape* caught fire, the burning ship sought refuge in the Delaware Bay. Coast Guard cutters and other vessels rallied to assist those aboard the burning ship, and all but 1 of the 368 passengers and crew members aboard the *Lenape* were saved. The ship, however, was a total loss.[213]

On April 16, 1926, the Cape Henlopen Lighthouse tumbled down the dune, leaving a trail of rubble. *Courtesy of the Delaware Public Archives.*

The charred hull of the abandoned ship inspired a last-ditch effort to save the Cape Henlopen Lighthouse. According to the *Wilmington Sunday Morning Star*:

> *The scheme was to float the hull, tow it to a point off the Henlopen Light, fill it with cement and sink it, thus forming a bulwark or breakwater. Against this, it was hoped—and it was but a hope—the tide would pile sand, forming a buffer that would not only halt the erosion of the sand beneath the foundation of the light, but would create a current that would actually restore sand already cut away.* [214]

Army engineers scoffed at that idea, and a similar plan to use surplus World War I vessels to create an artificial breakwater to reduce the erosion of sand came to naught. On April 16, 1926, the *Milford Chronicle* reported, "Historic Cape Henlopen Lighthouse, on the Delaware Bay, two miles south of Lewes, crumbled and toppled into the sea shortly after noon on Tuesday [April 13]." [215] The loss of the lighthouse made rumrunners' tasks a little more difficult, but they continued to find their way past the cape to deposit their illegal booze on shore.

Hijacking the Bootleggers

"Rival Bootleggers Wage Open Warfare"
—Sunday Morning Star

Bootlegging had its hazards, not the least of which was law enforcement agents. In April 1922, bootleggers loaded a cargo of gin in Chester, Pennsylvania, on the Delaware River, just south of Philadelphia. Bootleggers had already sold much of the liquor to thirsty customers in Wilmington, and it would only take a short ride down the river to deliver the illicit alcohol. On Saturday, April 8, the rumrunner slid up the Christina River and docked at Wilmington. As several crew members stood guard, others left the boat to make arrangements to haul the gin away and deliver it to thirsty customers. A short time later, a truck drove up on the wharf, and the driver said, "Hurry up, and get that stuff up here." The guard on the boat asked, "Are you the man sent after the booze?" The man in the truck replied, "Sure." Without further delay, the crew members loaded the truck and drove it off. Sometime later, a truck with the owners of the gin arrived, only to find that their liquor, worth $1,500, had been stolen.[216]

The victims of the theft could not very well call the police and report that their illegal booze had been stolen. As time went on and organized gangs competed for their share of the hooch trade, rival mobsters would let the police do their dirty work for them. In December 1925, federal agents received a tip that a car loaded with one hundred gallons of high-quality bootleg liquor was traveling from Chester, Pennsylvania, to Delaware. Reportedly, the booze was being transported by one of the largest rumrunners, who was in cahoots with the wife of a bootlegger who was currently in prison. Under the headline, "Rival Bootleggers Wage Open Warfare," the *Sunday Morning Star* reported, "According to gossip among the bootleggers and their friends, it is said that the tip, concerning the transporting of this liquor, was given to the federal officials by another bootlegger."[217]

The tipsters apparently gave the Prohibition agents the exact route that the car carrying the booze was taking, and the federal officials were able to intercept the vehicle just south of Delaware's border with Pennsylvania. The two men in the car were arrested, and the hooch, concealed in various parts of the car, was confiscated. The *Sunday Morning Star* speculated, "Naturally, the public is wondering what disposition will be made of the case. Moreover, some speculation is expressed as to whether reprisals will carry into the territory of the opposition bootlegger and whether further arrests will be made by the federal authorities."[218]

Two years later, in January 1927, George A. Hill, the deputy Prohibition administrator for Delaware, reported that hijackers were a "class of bandits born of Prohibition" who preyed on booze runners operating in Delaware. Hill believed that these road pirates had stolen the illegal hooch from a number of bootleggers and had taken the illicit alcohol to Southern Delaware, where they posed as corrupt Prohibition agents peddling the confiscated booze. The residents of Sussex County were all too happy to buy the hooch, and Hill reported that there was no scarcity of alcohol in Southern Delaware during the Christmas season. According to the *Sunday Morning Star*, "Pseudo agents are also reported to have had 'good' liquor on sale, claiming that they confiscated the liquor in raids, but Administrator Hill is of the opinion that they now transferred their operations to Maryland."[219]

Several rumrunners who had been transporting illegal alcohol between Philadelphia and Baltimore reported that they were harassed by holdup men as they passed through Delaware. Knowing that the drivers of the vehicles hauling the bootleg booze were unable to report the illegal hijacking of their cargo to the authorities, the hijackers operated without fear of prosecution. Instead of taking the booze, sometimes, the hijackers would offer to allow the bootleggers to keep their hooch for a generous price. Other hijackers would not only appropriate all of the liquor, but they would also take any money, personal valuables and even the vehicles of the bootleggers who were left penniless by the side of the road.[220]

The attacks on bootleggers became so common that they began to add extra armed men to their posses to protect the booze. After a Wilmington bootlegger received an order for hooch from a group in Baltimore, he became suspicious when the Baltimoreans wanted the delivery to take place in a secluded area in north Wilmington, near Shellpot Park. After the bootlegger loaded his truck with the booze, he added several of his friends with the appropriate firearms to his delivery posse. When the bootlegger arrived at the meeting place, the Baltimoreans proved to indeed be hijackers, and they were greatly surprised when the friends of the bootlegger emerged from the truck with guns drawn. Having turned the tables on the hijackers, the bootleggers stole all of the hijackers' cash, reported to amount to $1,200, and other valuables before sending them on their way.[221]

Not all the liquor that was hijacked was from rival gangs. Sometimes, rumrunners lost their booze to ordinary citizens who were their allies. A

Two captured rumrunners, the *Don* and the *Daisy-T*, sit at anchor in the canal at Lewes, at the base of Memorial Park. *Courtesy of the Delaware Public Archives.*

heavy fog was drifting over the waters off Cape Henlopen, at the entrance to Delaware Bay, when the rumrunner *Correllis* picked its way through the mist. The *Correllis* resembled two other booze boats, the *Don* and the *Daisy-T*, that had been captured earlier. All three vessels had low, narrow hulls with minimal superstructure. Only a small pilothouse and a raised cowling interrupted the smooth top deck that was unencumbered by railings or decorations. Several small portholes in the cowling gave the bootleggers stationed below the top deck a view of other approaching vessels, which enabled them to determine whether the vessels were friendly or not. The clean silhouette of the *Correllis* made it hard to see, and at the same time, it provided ample room to stow an estimated nineteen thousand bags of liquor divided into several hundred cases. Driven by a powerful engine, the *Correllis* steered through the fog the week before Thanksgiving in 1931.[222]

As the *Correllis* made its way past Cape Henlopen, the Delaware Breakwater and Lewes, the rumrunner continued up the bay until it reached Slaughter Beach, about four miles west of Milford and an all-important connection with the Du Pont Boulevard. (Local legend has it that Slaughter Beach got its name from some grisly incident during colonial times, but more likely, it acquired its grim moniker from the family name of local farmers.) During Prohibition, bootleggers worked in concert with local residents to stake out a plot in the water where the rumrunning boats would throw out heavily weighted cases of booze at high tide. There, the booze would sink to the bay's muddy bottom. At low tide, after the rumrunners had left the area, the local accomplices would retrieve the hooch from the shallow water and load the booze into trucks that would carry the alcohol upstate to its destination.[223]

As the bootleggers aboard the *Correllis* made their way toward Slaughter Beach in the thick fog, they were spotted by two Coast Guard patrol boats. Seeing the approaching Coast Guard vessels, the rumrunners steered close to shore and began to throw the cases of liquor overboard. As the last cases were dumped from the boat, most of the crew abandoned the *Correllis* and worked their way to shore. In the meantime, a crowd from Milford and Slaughter Neck, perhaps on the alert for the expected delivery of booze, had gathered on the beach near the place where the hooch had been jettisoned. The eager throng waded out to retrieve the submerged liquor. Some used oyster and clam rakes to locate the booze, and some simply waded until their nimble toes hit the bags of hooch. An estimate fifty cases of bootleg alcohol had been retrieved by the time the Coast Guard arrived. The appearance of the Coast Guard and other law enforcement officers led to a free-for-all, as government officials attempted to disperse the crowd, which was determined to take in as much booze as possible. Finally, the Coast Guard crew began to fire over the heads of the hooch hunters, who dispersed and left the area. Several men involved in the melee were arrested, but they were given a warning and quickly released. The Coast Guard dredged the water where the booze had been dumped and was able to retrieve four hundred cases of alcohol. Two of the crewmen who had remained on the *Correllis* were arrested, but they were also released on the grounds that there was no liquor on the boat at the time they were apprehended. The *Correllis*, however, was confiscated and taken to Lewes.[224]

On January 5, 1932, several men were pumping the rumrunner's oily bilge water into the Lewes and Rehoboth Canal when someone tossed a lit cigarette onto the oil slick that covered the water around the *Correllis*. The canal immediately burst into flames. For a short time, that entire section of the canal was ablaze, with flames that reached as high as the rooftops of nearby buildings. Those aboard the *Correllis* scurried ashore to escape the flames, and Coast Guard personnel were able to extinguish the fire before anyone was hurt. The rumrunners had lost their boat, and they had their cargo hijacked thanks to the alert and nimble-toed residents of Slaughter Neck.[225]

YES, DEAR

I had one foot over the door still to step forward when a shotgun was fired from
the head of the stairway, directly at the top of my head.
—*Edwin Totten, federal Prohibition agent*

"A few words about washing," the Lewes newspaper *Breakwater Light* commented in 1873, "put your clothes in a good suds the day before washing; in the morning, wash out of the water, warming it by the addition of hot water if desirable; put into boiling water, let them boil ten or fifteen minutes; wash out of the boiled suds with the hands; rinse, hang out and dry."[226]

Washing clothes, along with cooking, cleaning and raising the children was one of the back-breaking, time-consuming tasks that women performed one hundred years ago, but in the early twentieth century, things began to change. In 1917, the Wilmington and Philadelphia Traction Company ran a large advertisement in the Wilmington *Evening Journal* for the Thor Electric Washing Machine and Wringer. The advertisement gloated, "The Thor Electric Washing Machine does a washing of any size without hard work or worry....Not only washes—wrings. Costs only two cents an hour for electricity. Saves wear and tear on clothes because it washes without rubbing. Saves work for a woman. Saves wages for washday help."[227] As more and more homes became electrified, additional labor-saving appliances, including electric refrigerators, ovens and vacuum cleaners began appearing in Delaware homes. On May 1, 1927, the *Sunday Morning Star* commented:

> *Electricity as the servant of woman has established itself permanently in the home. Electrical heating pads replace the old-time hot bottles. There's the percolator, the waffle iron, the broiler, the toaster, sewing machine, curling iron, bottle warmers, heaters, pressers and ironers, vibrators, egg beaters, hair dryers, violet ray machine, fans, ventilators—in fact, there's an electrical device for practically every home use.*[228]

Aside from the violet ray machine, a popular but useless home medical instrument that featured a small glowing tube and produced a mild electric shock when the tube was touched to the skin, these devices lessened the burden of household chores, and more women sought work outside the home, including in bootlegging.[229]

In 1926, United States marshal George Stauffer of Cleveland complained that the number of women convicted of bootlegging charges was costing the federal government thousands of dollars, with little apparent benefit. There were few retraining or rehabilitation programs available for imprisoned women, who spent their time swapping stories about their illegal activities.[230] In the First State, men convicted of booze crimes were frequently given a warning, a fine and very little jail time, but women, often the wives or girlfriends of the bootleggers, received even lighter sentences.

In the early days of Prohibition, Edwin Totten recalled an incident that inadvertently involved the wife of a suspected bootlegger. He and a half-dozen other Prohibition agents were investigating reports of bootlegging activity east of Milford. Totten suspected that there was a still being operated by a man named Larry Smith on a large farm in the thinly populated area near the Delaware Bay. When the agents went to Smith's house, they encountered two women in the kitchen. The officers told them what they suspected and read them a search warrant. One of the women, who Totten presumed was Smith's wife, said that he was not home.[231]

Totten decided to take a look around, and he opened a doorway that led from the kitchen to a small hallway and a staircase that led to the second story of the house. The Prohibition agent recalled in the series he wrote for the *Wilmington Sunday Morning Star*, "My past experience had taught me to look before I stepped into a room, before entering, and probably, the small pause which I made saved me from death. I had one foot over the door still to step forward when a shotgun was fired from the head of the stairway, directly at the top of my head." The shotgun tore a hole in the floor between Totten's feet, but luckily, only a few of the shotgun pellets grazed Totten's head. Totten immediately stepped back into the kitchen and held a council of war with the other agents. They all wanted to capture the man who was wielding the shotgun, but none of the agents wanted to rush up the narrow staircase. They decided to use Smith's wife as a harrier to flush him out. She agreed to try to convince him to come down, provided that the agents would not harm him.[232]

As these negotiations were going on, Smith climbed out of a second-story window and dropped to the ground; still clutching his shotgun, he took off running. One of the agents saw him and gave chase. As the other agents came out of the house, Smith dropped to one knee, aimed and fired. One of the law enforcement officers was stung in the leg by the some of the pellets, but he was not seriously injured. Smith again took off running. Totten recalled, "We fired several shots in his general direction as he left but did not shoot to hit him, as he would have been struck in the back had we shot him, and it would have been difficult indeed to prove that it was in self-defense."[233]

Smith disappeared into the woods, and Totten's men gave up the chase. Some time later, Smith was captured by the state police and pled guilty to an assault charge. He was fined $300 and sentenced to five months in the workhouse. A year later, he was arrested and charged with possession of illegal alcohol. Smith was fined $100 and put on parole for two years. Neither of the two women in Smith's house were charged.[234]

Mrs. Smith assumed a passive role in the shootout at her farm, but other women were more actively involved in the bootlegging business. In August 1925, four Wilmington city detectives raided a house on Maple Street, and when they entered the house, they heard someone in the cellar. One of the detectives went to investigate, and while he was still on the staircase, he spotted Alexandra Krajewski filling a quart container from a pipe that was attached to a barrel of whisky that was buried three and a half feet below the earthen floor of the basement. The barrel could have been quickly covered with dirt when not in use. The detective at the top of the stairs called out to Krajewski, "Just leave it right there and go on upstairs." Mistaking the voice for her husband's, she replied, "Yes, dear," and went upstairs, where she was arrested.[235]

Not only were Delaware women actively involved in the bootlegging busines, but some of them aggressively defended the moonshiners. In August 1925, Wilmington police learned that Fran Kapaczal's saloon at Lord and Church Streets was serving something stronger than coffee and soda. A squad of six detectives was formed to raid Kapaczal's establishment, and the law enforcement officers packed into a car and drove to the suspected speakeasy. Anthony Merkowicz and his wife, Sophia, happened to be on the sidewalk in front of the saloon as the agents' car pulled up. Apparently, Anthony and Sophia were patrons of the speakeasy and feisty defenders of illegal booze. When the detectives dislodged from their car, they were immediately recognized by Anthony and Sophia, who attempted to grab them before they entered the saloon. While two of the detectives were left to battle Anthony and Sophia, the other officers ran into the saloon, where they arrested Kapaczal and confiscated a quantity of booze. The Merkowicz couple continued to put up a good a good fight, and the scuffle attracted a large crowd, who appeared to support Sophia and Anthony. When the other officers returned outside, they drew their weapons and intimidated the crowd into submission. In the fight, the *Sunday Morning Star* reported, "no one was seriously injured, but for a time, many blows were exchanged." Kapaczal was charged with violating the state liquor laws, and Anthony and Sophia were charged with assault and battery on the officers.[236]

A year after Sophia Merkowicz attacked the detectives in front of Kapaczal's saloon, the police raided a saloon in Wilmington on Bird Street. After four patrolmen entered the saloon, they attempted round up several men who were drinking there. As they did so, a heavy-set woman, believed to be the wife of the proprietor of the saloon, started to go down the stairs that led to the basement. The police sergeant told her to stop; she hesitated and continued down the steps. The sergeant wrapped his arms around the women's neck, but that did not slow her down. With the sergeant hanging on to her, she smashed several glass containers of whisky. Finally, a patrolman came to the sergeant's assistance; the sergeant was disentangled from the woman, and she was eventually subdued. The *Wilmington Sunday Star* reported, "When the officers finally returned, their clothing was not only torn, but they had the appearances of having been used to mop up the cellar floor." No arrests were made. The police believed that they had done enough damage for the night, and no liquor survived the smashing of the bottles that could have been used as evidence.[237] The Delaware women were not as infamous as their male counterparts, but they stood by their men and defended their booze.

PUSSYFOOTING DAYS ARE GONE

Romanism and Rum

*They smoke, they swear, they swagger like men into a barber shop and ask for
boyish bobs!*
—*Clarence True Wilson*

"For nearly ten years, fear seems to have gripped nearly everybody when
Prohibition has been mentioned," the Wilmington *Sunday Morning Star*
editorialized on June 17, 1928. The newspaper contended that some people
privately questioned the success of Prohibition, but they seldom spoke out
in public. Although the banning of alcohol was popular in Delaware when
Prohibition began, the newspaper argued that public sentiment in the
First State had changed. "For several years, people have been looking the
subject in the face, and the longer they looked, the more they learned of
the truth of the situation." In the same issue of the *Sunday Morning Star*, the
newspaper reported the results of a massive survey of Delaware residents
about their feelings on Prohibition, which ignited a renewed debate on
the wisdom of the "Noble Experiment." According to the newspaper, the
"pussyfooting days are gone."[238]

The survey was conducted by Pierre S. du Pont, an early opponent of
Prohibition and the leader of the Delaware division of the Association
Against the Prohibition Amendment. The questionnaire was mailed to

100,000 Delaware voters out of a population of about 225,000 residents of all ages, and it contained six questions, including: "Do you believe that much harm results for the abuse of drink under the prohibition laws?… Do you believe that alcoholic liquors…may now be bought, illegally, but freely?…Do you believe that the general disregard of prohibition laws is leading to other lawlessness?" The survey generated 37,951 replies. Although du Pont's questionnaire did not follow modern sophisticated statistical standards, he maintained:

> *The overwhelming affirmative answer to these six questions means nothing more than general dissatisfaction with the laws as now worded and enforced. After ten years of prohibition, alcoholic liquors may still be bought freely; much harm results from abuse of drink notwithstanding its prohibition, and the general disregard of the laws is such as to lead to other lawlessness—such is the verdict of 90% of those who have answered the questionnaire.*[239]

For the first eight years of Prohibition, the wet forces had been relatively quiet, but the du Pont survey gave them ammunition to raise the battle cry to make intoxicating beverages legal again. This, in turn, gave renewed energy to the dry forces. On March 31, 1928, Clarence True Wilson, the Milton native who was a leader in the drive to ratify the Eighteenth Amendment, gave a rousing address from the pulpit of the Union Methodist Episcopal Church at Fifth and Washington Streets in Wilmington. Complaining that some supporters of Prohibition bewailed that the amendment and the Volstead Act did not accomplish enough, Wilson bellowed, "If the only accomplishment of prohibition had been the destruction of the liquor traffic in this nation, that would be vindication enough to establish it as the greatest moral accomplishment of the age.…Prohibition has done more to clean up politics than any one thing in the modern age."[240]

Wilson recalled a time when "drunken senators and representatives sprawled in the seats of our capitol; when there was a barroom at both ends of that great marble structure." Shifting gears a bit, he spoke of the days before Prohibition, when saloons lined the streets of Wilmington, Philadelphia and other cities. According to Wilson, these saloons profited by "the selling [of liquor] to minors; the harboring of women; the violating of the midnight closing law. Despite the twittering about hip flask, don't be deceived, our boys are not drinking half of what was drunk when minors were sold liquor." Wilson also traced the economic success of the 1920s to

A flapper whose high boots could easily conceal a flask of illegal whiskey. *Courtesy of the Library of Congress.*

the banning of alcohol. "Prosperity is due almost entirely to the institution of prohibition following the war; when other nations were wrecked, as industries always are after a war and always were for us after former wars, we enjoyed prosperity such as never known before."[241]

In passing, Dr. Wilson decried the changing status of women, particularly the flappers who wore short, loose-fitting skirts and flaunted social conventions. To Wilson, they were a "feather-brained set of imitators of men, who pack up all the vices and none of the virtues of the male sex. They smoke, they swear, they swagger like men into a barber shop and ask for boyish bobs! 'Give me a boyish bob,' they say, as if they were not satisfied to be the girls God made them. Those bobs may not be a sin, but they look like sin."[242]

A reason behind the uptick in rhetoric about Prohibition was that 1928 was a presidential election year, and the battle lines were clearly drawn. Republicans generally favored Prohibition and keeping the country dry, so they nominated the incumbent, President Herbert Hoover. Democrats, who had had enough of Prohibition and who wanted to return to the good old wet days, selected New York governor Al Smith as their standard-bearer. When a Republican National Committee committeewoman urged the committee to release a circular letter that told women to "save the United States from being Romanized and rum-ridden," Hoover was quick to disavow the slur against the Catholic Smith.[243] But the damage had been done, and Smith's religion became an underlying issue in the race. Although the du Pont survey had indicated that there was strong support for modification or outright repeal of Prohibition, Hoover was riding a wave of prosperity, and he and many other Republicans won in a landslide victory in November. Despite the du Pont survey that indicated voters in Delaware were opposed to Prohibition, Hoover, an avowed dry, carried the state with a whopping 66 percent of the vote.[244]

In an analysis of the election season by Rehoboth's *Delaware Coast News*, the newspaper contended:

> *The extensive use of the radio in the past* [presidential] *campaign has given practically all the people an opportunity of hearing the candidates discuss the issues. The candidates, instead of being far-off, legendary figures, became real-live, close, familiar persons when their voices issued from the multitudinous number of loud speakers the country over.*[245]

In the waning years of the nineteenth century, Guglielmo Marconi developed a rudimentary radio system that was capable of transmitting only the dots and dashes of Morse code. Initially dubbed a "wireless telegraph," Marconi's invention continued to be improved, and by the mid-1920s, radio stations were broadcasting to an ever-increasing number of home receivers.

Early consumer radios were powered by several batteries, the speakers were separate from the receivers and the receivers contained a collection of vacuum tubes that took a budding electronic wizard to operate. In November 1926, the Wilmington *Sunday Morning Star* headlined, "No Home Complete Without Radio."[246] The next month, the newspaper published an article titled "Helpful Tips for That New Radio Set." It advised:

> *Plug in the speaker, and with one tube only, or an old one of the same type that will light, try out each one of the sockets in turn and observe what happens when the filament of the tube is lighted. If the tube properly lights in each socket, the new tubes may be placed in the sockets, and the*

> *receiver is ready to operate....Tune the receiver according to the directions furnished with it, remembering that a station cannot be heard unless it is broadcasting...Practice tuning-in the local stations, do not "fish" for distance until you become better acquainted with the tuning operations.*[247]

Over the next two years, dramatic improvements to home radios made them easier to operate. House currents replaced the batteries, and generally, the average person did not have to tinker with the vacuum tubes. Atwater Kent, an early manufacturer of dependable and easy-to-use radios, advertised in the *Delaware Coast News*:

> *Atwater Kent Radio is a wise investment because it gives you fine radio at a lower price. You can't get greater dependability....Out of the many stations that the greater power of Model 40 brings you, the Full-Vision Dial quickly selects whatever you want—politics, dance music, classics, famous singers and actors, travel, lectures, adventure. You never worry about electric current. It comes from the light socket and costs only a fraction of a cent an hour.*[248]

When candidates for state and federal offices took to the airwaves, they tended to tone down some of their rhetoric. According to the *Delaware Coast News*, "The speakers, knowing well that their voices would be heard throughout the length and breadth of the land, have weighed their utterances carefully and taken pains to deliver addresses marked by high-mindedness and intellectuality."[249] The use of the radio may have caused a temporary pause in the traditional mudslinging and name-calling, but when it came to Prohibition, the "high-mindedness and intellectuality" of the public discourse only increased as the drive to make Delaware wet again gathered new strength.

BOOTLEG FRATERNITY

He was welcomed as a fraternity brother and showed no compunction about drinking the other's stuff.
—Sunday Morning Sun

As the Christmas season approached in 1928, organized bootleg mobsters were waging open warfare in Philadelphia, Baltimore and other cities near Delaware. The gang conflict resulted in the deaths of police officers, innocent bystanders, bootleggers and hijackers. Wilmington did not see a similar level of violence, but despite the efforts of law enforcement officials, the Delaware city was well supplied with liquor. The stepped-up efforts of the Coast Guard resulted in the capture of several rumrunning vessels, but many of the boats laden with illegal booze got through and enabled Wilmington residents to stock up for the holiday season. The ample supply of booze also kept prices low. According to the *Sunday Morning Star*, Bacardi rum was selling around $110 a case, blended rye could be had for $65 a case and Champagne was going for $115 a case. The largest variation in prices was seen with scotch. If imported from Canada, it went for $110 a case, but if it was brought in from the Bahamas, it was selling for a bargain $65 a case. The ample supply of booze and the stability of prices led the *Sunday Morning Star* to comment, "Now that the prices are known, approximately, at least, it is not to be doubted that all of the thirsty will rush out immediately and lay in the Christmas supply, that is, all who have the price and the private bootlegger."[250]

According to the newspaper, the reason the prices remained stable was that the Wilmington bootleggers formed a loose, friendly "fraternity," as opposed to the rival gangs that were prevalent in other cities. The *Sunday Morning Star* noted, "Although the fraternity has no officers and is not organized in the recognized term of organization, it is carried out as forcefully as though it had. The functioning is carried out in the form of social work, which keeps them in close contact with each other and permits them to compare notes and to warn each other of possible raids."[251] It was customary for most Wilmington speakeasies to close around midnight, but a few remained open until around 3:00 a.m. to accommodate their fellow bootleggers, who tended to be lavish spenders. When a *Star* reporter visited a speakeasy, the bootlegger told him that he was closing up but that he would take the writer to another place that remained open for a few more hours. From around midnight until 3:00 a.m., the bootlegger, with the reporter in tow, visited about six different places, where, according to the *Star*, "He was welcomed as a fraternity brother and showed no compunction about drinking the other's stuff." The bootleggers had no reluctance in discussing who might be due for a raid. They exchanged notes on habitual drunks and rowdies who should be kept out of their speakeasies because their behavior attracted the attention of the police.[252]

While bootleggers continued to operate freely in Delaware, members of the Woman's Christian Temperance Union continued to lobby the public

The WCTU fountain still stands next to the Rehoboth Beach Boardwalk. *Photograph by Michael Morgan.*

The weather-worn plaque on the WCTU fountain greets thirsty beachgoers. *Photograph by Michael Morgan.*

This photograph was taken a just few years after the WCTU fountain (*left of center, next to the boat*) was erected and shows that it was already popular. *Courtesy of the Delaware Public Archives.*

against the evils of alcohol. As part of a long-standing national campaign, the Rehoboth chapter of the WCTU sponsored a cafeteria-style lunch at the Epworth ME Church. The menu for the April 1929 affair included meatloaf, waffles, hot rolls, deviled eggs, potato salad, pickles, cake and pie.[253] The money raised by the lunch helped defer the cost of a drinking fountain that was erected later that year at the end of Rehoboth Avenue and the boardwalk.

While the WCTU was busy making plans for its Rehoboth fountain (which became a resort landmark), the stock market crashed in October 1929, signaling the economic collapse that would culminate in the Great Depression. In Delaware, the most immediate effects of the economic downturn were felt in Wilmington, where its urban economy was more tightly bound with the commercial markets of the Northeast. Outside of Wilmington, the rural parts of the state retained a mostly agrarian economy that had not shared in the boom of the roaring 1920s or the bust of the stock market crash. In Sussex County, farmers had raised tobacco, grain, peaches, strawberries and other crops as they adapted to altering conditions over the years. The farmers of rural Delaware raised much of their own food, and a number of stores, including Sussex County's only hospital, sometimes accepted chickens, eggs, milk and other produce in lieu of cash. At the beginning of the twentieth century, Charles Jones, a fertilizer salesman, was familiar with many farming families in the southern part of the state, where holly trees grew as high as sixty feet. Jones was a frequent visitor to Burton's store on Federal Street in Milton, where he observed farmers bartering homemade holly wreaths for household goods, and Jones was convinced that the holly wreath business was a golden opportunity. Ignoring the comments of his doubting wife, Jones, armed with the slogan—"Quality is remembered when price is forgotten"— quickly built a network of local farmers for whom the manufacture of holly wreaths became the last cash crop of the season and helped them weather some of the darkest days of the Great Depression.[254]

Southern Delaware farmers were also insulated from some of the economic hardships of the Great Depression through the development of the broiler industry. In 1923, the economy of Southern Delaware changed again when Cecile Steele received a shipment of chickens. The Ocean View resident used her chickens to produce eggs, and she normally received a brood of fifty chicks. When five hundred young birds arrived, Steele decided to raise the chickens and sell them when they reached two pounds. Steele received sixty-two cents per pound for her chickens, and the next year, she sold one thousand birds. Impressed by her success, many of Steele's neighbors began raising chickens, and by the time that the stock market crashed, Sussex County was the center of the lucrative broiler industry.[255] Finally, many out-of-work Delaware residents were more willing to participate in bootlegging as a way to supplement their income.

LOOK AT THE CHRISTMAS I COULD HAVE HAD!

The boat hit a sandbar, and the crew threw overboard many cases of liquor in order to make the load lighter.
—Delaware Coast News

By November 1930, it had been over a year since the stock market had crashed, and the growing effects of the Great Depression continued to worsen in Delaware. The public eye began to turn away from Prohibition and focused, instead, on the worsening economic conditions. On the Delaware Coast, the experience of the previous decade had taught the rumrunners many lessons on how to avoid capture by the Coast Guard, which, in turn, had learned many of the bootleggers' tricks. The cat-and-mouse game played by law enforcement and moonshiners sometimes had unexpected and occasionally humorous outcomes that indicated the way the residents of Southern Delaware thought about Prohibition.

There was only a sliver of a moon showing on November 22, 1930, and the waters around Cape Henlopen at the mouth of the Delaware Bay were dark. The rumrunners liked it that way. Despite the floundering economy, the residents of the coastal region of the First State were preparing for Thanksgiving, and many children were looking past the Thursday feast for the appearance of the first Christmas decorations. In the murky waters around the cape, a sixty-foot-long rumrunner, loaded with cases of holiday booze, headed into the bay. The bootleggers were confident that their vessel's four-hundred-horsepower engine would enable them to outrun any of the Coast Guard's patrol boats. Cruising around the stone barriers of the Delaware Breakwater, the small boat continued past Lewes. Two centuries earlier, pirates from Captain Kidd's ship had secretly navigated the same waters, and like Kidd, the bootleggers aboard the twentieth-century boat also wanted to avoid any contact with the lawful authorities.[256]

The clear waters of the bay seemed open for the small boat as it chugged forward. The crewmen kept a close watch on the waters around them, but they should have been more concerned with what lay beneath their boat. Suddenly, the men were nearly knocked off their feet. According to the *Delaware Coast News*, "The boat hit a sand bar, and the crew threw overboard many cases of liquor in order to make the load lighter." After 150 cases of illegal booze had been pitched into the bay, the bootleggers' boat was light enough to slide off the sandbar. The rumrunners quickly made their way to shore, where they deposited the remaining cases of liquor into an abandoned shack. The bootleggers dashed to the mouth of Lewes Creek, where they turned in to one of the streams that flowed from the Great Marsh. The Coast Guard patrol boat was unable to negotiate the narrow channels of the marsh, giving the rumrunners time to hide their cargo in the wetlands.[257]

Meanwhile, the authorities got wind of the bootleggers' activities, and a patrol boat headed out of Coast Guard Base No. 9 at Cape May,

New Jersey. The rumrunners, however, abandoned their boat, which was picked up by the Coast Guard, who also spent the night fishing out of the bay the booze that had been tossed overboard to lighten the boat when it was on the sandbar. The crew of the patrol boat had picked up between 140 and 175 cases of the liquor, all encased in bags, from the bay by Sunday morning.[258]

As the Coast Guard searched the bay for the hooch, a seaplane landed off Rehoboth on Sunday morning; it was carrying a U.S. marshal who was there to help with the investigation of the case. However, no trace of the crew of the rumrunner could be found. The gang was believed to have been the same one that landed a boatload of illegal whiskey in a marsh along the Mispillion River near Milford nearly a week before. Two truckloads, which were believed to be only part of that cargo, were captured by the state police. On Tuesday morning, around 7:00 a.m., another apparent rumrunner appeared off Rehoboth Beach, going at a slow pace, as if the crew was uncertain of where to land. Within a few minutes, a Coast Guard patrol boat rounded Cape Henlopen and bore down on the rumrunner. The bootleggers, however, spotted the Coast Guard boat, and the moonshiners turned east and headed out to sea.[259]

The bootlegging activity in late November 1930, was part of an annual invasion of rumrunners who arrived in the weeks between Thanksgiving and Christmas with illegal liquor for the holiday season. Most coastal residents were busy preparing for the upcoming holidays, and holly wreaths, Christmas trees and other decorations would soon appear on many homes. Shoppers would begin going out on expeditions to buy presents, and cooks would be busy in the kitchen, baking cookies, cakes and other goodies for the holidays. The Coast Guard had seized the abandoned boat and fished most of the jettisoned alcohol out of the Delaware Bay.[260] Some of the illegal alcohol had been stashed in a small shanty. A short time later, a duck hunter from Lewes happened upon the shanty. He was about to enter the shack when he decided against it and continued on his way. Shortly after the duck hunter left, members of the Coast Guard arrived, discovered the shack and confiscated the cache of alcohol. When the duck hunter learned that he had missed a shanty full of booze, he moaned, "Look at the Christmas I could have had!"[261]

NEW SHERIFF IN TOWN:
THREE-GUN WILSON ARRIVES

Prohibition law enforcement should be carried on by men who are possessed with aggressive enthusiasm and genuine convictions.
—Harold "Three-Gun" Wilson

When Harold D. Wilson came to Southern Delaware, he had a hard-boiled reputation, a slick nickname and a fervent spirit for law enforcement. With the exception of sharing a last name, Harold was not related to Clarence True Wilson, another vocal antiliquor advocate. A combination of the fiery Billy Sunday and the untouchable Elliot Ness, Harold was determined to rally the people of Delaware and enforce the Prohibition laws. He was born in Cawker City, a dwindling town of less than one thousand residents in north-central Kansas, in 1884, when old-timers could still recall the hardships of living on the frontier. When he was still a child, Wilson's family moved to Shelburne Falls, Massachusetts, where his mother died when he was twelve years old. After working his way through Tufts College near Boston, Wilson appeared to be on a bookish career path, as he worked as a reporter, editor and publisher, but that path was interrupted by World War I and a stint as an army aviator. After Prohibition began, Wilson was appointed to the Chief Prohibition Enforcement Office in Massachusetts.[262]

HAROLD DAVID WILSON

Despite his scholarly appearance, Harold "Three-Gun" Wilson was a hard-driving crusader against alcoholic beverages. *From* Dry Laws and Wet Politicians.

On December 20, 1921, Wilson was in his office when an agent rushed in and exclaimed, "Chief, the lid's off in the Quincy House. All the Republican politicians in the state are crammed into a…barroom trying to see who can last the longest. It is a regular old-time drinking carousal." Wilson later recalled:

> *For a moment, it all seemed to me a poignant tragedy that practically all the political leaders of the Republican Party, my own party, should be gathered tighter in a public place, openly flouting the Constitution of the United States. I was so disgusted at this monumental hypocrisy that*

123

nothing could have stood in the way of my raiding that banquet. I could
see clearly, however, that such a raid meant the beginning of the end for me
as prohibition chief.

Determined to enforce the liquor laws at whatever the cost, Wilson turned
to his two agents and said, "Boys, it probably means your jobs. Are you with
me?" They answered, "You bet. Let's go.'"[263]

When Wilson raided the Quincy House, he discovered that the liquor
was flowing freely, and he arrested a number of high-ranking associates of
the governor of Massachusetts. As he predicted, the politicians were out
for his scalp. Forced to resign as a Prohibition enforcement agent, Wilson
continued his crusade against illegal booze in Pittsburgh, and he used his
literary talents to write *Dry Laws and Wet Politicians*, which justified his actions
in Massachusetts.

Wilson believed in agents who were dedicated to Prohibition and the
enforcement of the liquor laws, and in *Dry Laws and Wet Politicians*, he wrote,

> *Prohibition law enforcement should be carried on by men who are possessed*
> *with aggressive enthusiasm and genuine convictions relative to the cause*
> *of prohibition. In addition to conviction and enthusiasm, agents must be*
> *able to stand the gaff of public opinion....Physical bravery is a wonderful*
> *asset, but it is not to be compared to the mental poise that can carry on when*
> *in the right, regardless of the consequences.*[264]

Accused of being a publicity hound, it was said that Wilson acquired the
nickname "Three-Gun" when he was given a pair of pistols by an admirer,
adding it to the one that he already carried. In the preface to another of
Wilson's books, *Dry Law Facts Not Fiction*, Reverend James W. Colona wrote
that the sobriquet came about because Wilson was "a triple threat to all the
violators and nullifiers of the laws of the state and nation." First, Wilson
was "an enforcement raider, energetic, daring and relentless." Second, he
commanded attention when he spoke or wrote, and his "utterly fearless
exposures of the lawlessness of the forces of evil are increasingly breaking
up the iniquitous business of liquor law violation." Third, "his buoyant
enthusiasm and indefatigable industry in his task of law enforcement
are contagious."[265]

However he acquired his nickname, Wilson wore it proudly. He believed
that news of the arrest of prominent people for liquor violations was often
suppressed, and to counter this, Wilson once wrote:

Pussyfooting Days Are Gone

Enforcement that can be concealed under a bushel basket is not enforcement at all. The only raids that can be suppressed, as far as the newspapers are concerned, are the picayune pink tea affairs in which the bootleggers are notified in advance. Gently slap a booze hound on the wrist and apologize for molesting him, and the press will accommodate the "pols" by refraining from any mention of the pathetic pretense at enforcement. Grab the contemptible treacherous poison hooch vender by the nape of the neck and the seat of the pants and throw him into jail where he belongs, and nothing in the world can prevent publicity.[266]

After ten years of his somewhat bland prosecution of the Prohibition laws in Delaware, fiery Three-Gun Wilson was appointed a Prohibition enforcement agent for Delaware. It immediately became apparent that a new sheriff was in town when Wilson proclaimed:

When I came to Delaware late in September 1930…that publicity was the only weapon with which such a [Prohibition enforcement] *campaign could be imitated and that I intended to use it to the best of my ability.… The man who set the pace in a publicity campaign is a target for all kinds of abuse. I have and am receiving plenty. In some quarters, I have been termed the most unpopular man in the state. I glory in this unpopularity. It is the reward for being a "fool" crusading prohibitionist. I have set a goal and intend to hew to the line, let the chips fall where they may.[267]*

According to Wilson, the enforcement of the Prohibition laws in Delaware required cooperation among the various law enforcement agencies and the support of the public. Wilson believed, "Public support is lacking, not because the American people are inherently lawless or because majority opinion is against enforcement, but because the public is confused, discouraged and totally lacking in facts as to the true situation." In his opinion, if the government was to make progress in enforcing the liquor laws, the public needed to be informed of the functions of different law enforcement units and to understand "the type of filthy, lazy, desperado who is commercializing in liquor."[268]

To clear up confusion about Prohibition enforcement, Wilson proposed a series of meetings to make people aware of the situation, "Facts, pure ungarbled digestible facts, sustained by local authorities, are imperative."[269] Wilson also believed that the public needed to be informed of the activities of law enforcement efforts to control liquor on the local and state level.

Finally, he believed that a program of "defensive enforcement" that consisted of "unexpected inspections of clubs and hotels; public opinion, not search warrants, being the modus operandi in obtaining entrée at any time, a surprising large number of clubs and hotels being delighted to cooperate in this program."[270] He claimed that if the public cooperated with law enforcement authorities, it would be an easy matter to determine and shut down where booze was being peddled. "Any intelligent man can tell a barroom when he sees it, and any intelligent man ought to be able to recognize a speakeasy. Dingy, dimly-lighted dives with no visible means of support are speakeasies. It is not necessary to sample their wares any more than it is to bite a skunk to know a skunk."[271]

According to an editorial in the *Sunday Morning Star*, there were an estimated 500 speakeasies in Wilmington in 1928: "What it is remembered that before Prohibition, under the state license system, there were only 168 saloons, and that this number was all that was left out of about 240 a score of years earlier, the estimate of 500 ten years after Prohibition seems appalling." Wilson proposed surveying the state's general population to find out how many speakeasies were in Delaware, and in the meantime, he started cracking down on suspected speakeasies and bootleggers.[272]

On October 25, 1930, Wilson and another agent entered Malcom McCoy's cigar store on West Seventh Street in Wilmington without a search warrant. Passing through a set of swinging doors, Wilson attempted to grab McCoy, who broke free and went into a back room, where he picked up a bottle. As McCoy smashed the bottle on some of the steps that led to an alley, Wilson came up from behind and smacked him on the head with a blackjack. After Wilson struck McCoy, the agent remarked, "You will get rough with Three-Gun Wilson, will you?"[273]

After McCoy was arrested, Wilson picked up the neck of the broken bottle and was able to "pour" three or four drips into another bottle. Wilson also found a bit of liquid in the bottom of a glass and an ounce of liquid from another bottle, which were all mixed together. When they tasted that meager sample, the agents announced that it contained 2.75 percent alcohol.

Although Wilson claimed that the he had given McCoy a "love tap" with his blackjack, the *Sunday Morning Star* reported that McCoy's attorney said, "It is just such tactics as these—entering without a search warrant, using a blackjack before getting hands on a drop of liquor—that cusses some of the life and death tragedies of prohibition enforcement."[274]

The next weekend, Wilson, believing most of the Delaware Prohibition agents were known to the bootleggers, recruited agents from Philadelphia and

New Jersey. Some of these agents worked for several weeks and determined the locations of several Wilmington speakeasies. This time, Wilson obtained search warrants and raided over a half-dozen speakeasies and made twenty-three arrests, and in a pattern that Wilson would follow during his tenure as a Prohibition agent, he immediately gave a speech at St. Paul's Methodist Episcopal Church, in which he described those raids.[275]

Three-Gun Wilson's crackdown was not confined to Wilmington. He sent undercover agents into the southern part of the state, and in February 1931, they had gathered enough evidence to conduct raids on eight houses and gas stations in Delmar and Seaford. One of the men arrested had the prophetic name Isaac H. "Still" (from North Laurel). As the Prohibition agents raided Still's home, the alleged bootlegger dumped a large quantity of liquor onto the floor. Wilson's men attempted to mop up the liquor, but they doubted that they had recovered enough to charge Still. Still had been arrested several times in the past on liquor charges. Wilson declared that Charles W. Mitchell of Delmar was one of the

In 1931, Three-Gun Wilson raided Delmar, which sits astride the Delaware–Maryland border. *Courtesy of the Delaware Public Archives.*

kingpins of the liquor traffic in Southern Delaware. Mitchell was arrested in the part of Delmar known as "Frogtown," which Wilson characterized as a "hell hole." As was his habit, Wilson used these raids to speak at a mass meeting at the Methodist Episcopal Church at Delmar, and he took this opportunity to organize one of his Fact Finding and Law Supporting Committees for Delmar.[276]

After the raids on the western side of Sussex County, Wilson and his agents moved on to Lewes, where the *Sunday Morning Star* reported, "A 25-gallon still is said to have been found in operation in the home of George Showell….A large quantity of mash was also seized. Showell was not in the house to 'welcome' the agents, but the latter soon expect to apprehend him. The agents then raided the home of Rhoda Gunby…and found a small quantity of liquor."[277]

The Gunby home was across the street from the Lewes Auditorium, where Wilson gave a stirring speech before a packed house of several hundred people. He urged the formation of a Fact Finding and Law Supporting Committee that would report violators of the Prohibition laws. According to the *Delaware Coast News*, "Mr. Wilson stated that bootleggers were a very low type of person and that, in all of his ten years of experience as an enforcement officer, he had found them to be yellow and cowardly and undersized either mentally or physically."[278] Having made several arrests and after giving a rousing speech, Harold "Three-Gun" Wilson left Southern Delaware. A new sheriff was in town, but with all the bluster and publicity, did it really make a difference?

BOOZE ON THE BEACH

The Fenwick Island raid was considered by Federal officials to have been one of the largest hauls Coast Guardsmen in this district have made in several years.
—Delaware Coast News

In the early years of Prohibition, agent Edwin Totten maintained:

> *I have been offered numerous bribes, ranging from $10 to sums that reached four figures; I have been with other agents and officers when we were offered bribes and various inducements to overlook a violation. I have served with agents from Washington, general agents and special agents, as well as*

> *agents from other states, and several who were appointed and served in*
> *Delaware, and I have never known of a bribe being accepted, but I have*
> *known of efforts being made to bring an extra charge of bribery against*
> *these making the offer.*[279]

Although Totten claimed that he never knew of a bribe being accepted, that was naive, and bootleggers continued to offer them as long as Prohibition was in effect. There is no way of knowing how many bribes were accepted and went unreported. Several unsuccessful Delaware bribery attempts were documented in *Chesapeake Rumrunners of the Roaring Twenties* by Eric Mills. In August 1930, two men who said that they were from New Jersey approached a member of the Lewes Coast Guard Station and offered him a substantial amount of money to look the other way as they landed their illicit cargo. The enlisted man refused, and the bootleggers said they would land anyway on a more deserted stretch of the coast. The Coast Guardman reported the attempted bribe to his superiors, but the bootleggers were never caught.[280]

Over a year later, in November 1931, James Baker, who was in charge of the Indian River Inlet Coast Guard Station received a call from a man asking him to meet at the inlet, which was a short distance from the station. When Baker arrived at the inlet, he discovered four men in a car with New York plates. Although it was dark, Baker recognized one of the men as a notorious bootlegger known as "Smokey Joe." According to Mills, the bootleggers told Baker that a mothership carrying illegal liquor had arrived off the Delaware Coast and that the rumrunners wanted to land their booze in time for the Christmas season. The bootleggers knew that Baker's crew at the Coast Guard station north of the inlet kept a careful eye on that stretch of the coast, which, at that time, was nothing but barren dunes. As was the case in the Lewes bribery attempt, the bootleggers simply needed the Coast Guard to look the other way while their cargo was landed. When Baker heard what the rumrunners wanted (Baker and his crew would be rewarded for his inattention to duty), the Coast Guard officer flatly refused to cooperate. Frustrated by the conscientious Baker, the four rumrunners piled into their Chrysler and headed south toward Bethany Beach.[281]

A month later, Baker encountered another shifty character known as "Summers" who went by several aliases. Summers, whom Baker thought was an agent for a rumrunner from New Jersey or New York, offered the Coast Guard officer $500 a night if he and his crew found other things to do while the bootleggers landed a cargo of hooch on the beach, hauled it across

The Indian River Inlet Life-Saving Station has been restored and stands today as a museum dedicated the history of the Delaware Coast. *Photograph by Michael Morgan.*

the sand to the coastal bay, reloaded it onto scows and transported it to the mainland. Instead of dismissing the offer outright, Baker began to question Summer, who grew suspicious, jumped into his car and drove off.[282]

South of the Indian River Inlet stood the small beachfront community of Bethany Beach, and farther south lay Fenwick Island, which had a lighthouse, only a few winter inhabitants and an unpaved road that connected it to the mainland. The lighthouse gave bootleggers a handy navigation marker at night, the beach offered a dark landing place and the road provided a direct route to the mainland. In James D. Meehan's oral history of the Delaware Coast, *When Life Was a Day at the Beach,* Oliver Cropper recalled, "Fenwick Island was a loading place for alcohol. Chess Watson, a friend of mine, went to Philadelphia and I guess got in with the mob or something. Anyway, they started to bring whiskey right in to Fenwick Island. Rumrunners would hire teenage boys and give them twenty dollars a night to help unload whiskey."[283]

The beach at Fenwick Island was an inviting spot for landing bootleg booze. *Courtesy of the Delaware Public Archives.*

As the Great Depression wore on, the public's attention was focused on the worsening economic conditions, but for bootleggers, it was business as usual, and in October 1932, the rumrunners began to stock up for the holiday season. On October 2, the beacon of the Fenwick Island Lighthouse guided a rumrunning vessel to the southern Delaware Coast. Working with the military precision of an amphibious invasion, the bootleggers began to ferry cases of illegal booze from ship to shore. Within a short time, over 200 cases had been stacked on the dark and deserted sands of Fenwick Island. They soon had 219 cloth-covered metal containers filled with bootleg liquor stacked on the beach. The bootleggers, however, were not alone. Without warning, members of the Coast Guard and the Delaware State Police appeared and surrounded the bootleggers. Offshore, the rumrunners on the mothership sensed that something was wrong and sped away. Fourteen men on the beach were taken into custody, and the illegal alcohol was confiscated. According to the *Delaware Coast News*, "The Fenwick Island raid was considered by federal officials to have been one of the largest hauls Coast Guardsmen in this district have made in several years."[284]

Seven of the men who were arrested pleaded guilty to the possession and transportation of illegal alcohol, and the seven others entered pleas of not guilty and demanded a jury trial. At their trial, the defense attorneys argued that samples of the cases seized at Fenwick Island could not be introduced as evidence on the grounds that the government had failed to show a connection between the illegal liquor and the defendants. Although the men had been arrested next to the cases of illegal alcohol on an otherwise deserted beach, the judge ruled that the government had not demonstrated any connection between the accused and the booze. The judge directed the jury to return a verdict of not guilty, and the defendants were released.[285]

LAST CALL

They were a grim lot of marchers, but their spirits were high,
and they were far from depressed.
—Sunday Morning Star

The movement to ban alcoholic beverages began in the nineteenth century, and by the time Prohibition was enacted, there were several well-organized groups, including the Woman's Christian Temperance Union and the Anti-Saloon League, that advocated for the enforcement of the Volstead Act and the Delaware liquor laws. Those who opposed Prohibition were not as well organized, but when the ban on alcohol became reality, wets became more unified. The Association Against the Prohibition Amendment was founded in 1918 in a vain attempt to prevent the passage of the Eighteenth Amendment. After this defeat, the association remained active. The ill effects of Prohibition (organized crime, police corruption and a disrespect for law and order) gave new life to the association, and it grew throughout the 1920s. In Delaware, the association included members of the du Pont family.[286] In 1929, Pauline Morton Sabin, once a staunch supporter of Prohibition, founded the Women's Organization for National Prohibition Reform (WONPR), and by the end of 1931, it had 1.5 million members.[287]

The growing grassroots support for a change in Prohibition laws gained little traction during the prosperity of the 1920s. In 1928, Herbert Hoover ran on a platform to continue prohibition, but his campaign slogan, "A chicken in every pot and a car in every garage," indicated that he understood that the major issue was the roaring 1920s economy. When the stock market crashed in October 1929, Hoover's popularity and the fervor to enforce Prohibition laws crashed with it.

Members of the Women's Organization for National Prohibition Reform pose with two posters advocating for the repeal of the Eighteenth Amendment at a flying field near Milford. *Courtesy of the Delaware Public Archives.*

Over the years, the farmers of the First State had raised tobacco, grain, peaches, strawberries and other crops as they adapted to changing conditions, and the growth of the chicken market helped offset the declining economy, but the effects of the Great Depression began to be felt across Delaware. At that time, most efforts to help those who could not find work were conducted by a series of local committees, but these efforts proved ineffective, and the number of unemployed grew. By December 1931, with winter bearing down, many families faced the prospect of little food and no heat. On Saturday, December 5, 1931, a horde of one thousand marchers descended on Wilmington on their way to Washington, D.C., to present their grievances to Congress. Styled the "National Hunger March," they arrived in trucks and assembled outside Wilmington. Divided into detachments that were supervised by a designated captain, the marchers assembled on the northern edge of the city as groups of five abreast. Dressed in long coats, the men wore mostly flat workers' caps, but some sported fedoras. Each marcher wore a wristband marked, "National Hunger March," and it included the date, December 7. Led by a squad of motorcycle policemen and a car carrying the superintendent of public safety George Black, the marchers moved down North Market Street, carrying signs and banners with slogans reflecting their grievances: "Refuse Wage Cuts," "Free Milk for Workers' Children in the Schools," "No Sheriff Sales of Workers' Homes," "We Want Jobs, Not Soup," "We Have Produced the Wealth of This Country, Why Should We Starve Now?" "Tax the Rich to Feed the Unemployed." Here and there, mixed in with the marchers, were several Black workers and some signs that read, "No Discrimination Against Negroes." Although most of the marchers were men, several women were in their ranks, a few wearing raccoon coats. According to the *Sunday Morning Star*, "It was a motley crowd, noisy with shouts and songs, but orderly. They marched five abreast with what appeared to be an officer in charge of each detachment. Negro and white, both men and women, marched side by side."[288]

The marchers wound their way onto French Street as they passed through downtown Wilmington. As the marchers moved through the streets, they chanted slogans and sang several verses about the need for assistance to the tune of "Onward Christian Soldiers." According to the *Sunday Morning Star*, "They were a grim lot of marchers, but their spirits were high, and they were far from depressed. Most of them appeared to down-and-outers, but others had unmistakable signs of respectability about them. A goodly amount of women was sprinkled through the ranks, some of them with silk stockings, while one was wearing a raccoon coat."[289]

Along the parade route, crowds of onlookers lined the streets, and some spectators mumbled the marchers' plea for unemployment insurance, but these sympathetic cries were barely audible. There was little, if any, cheering. At Fourth and French Streets, a woman spectator give a few cheers, but the crowd did not respond. On Front Street, near King Street, a man rushed over to one of the leaders of the column and gave him a white carnation.[290]

Swinging back onto South Market Street, the marchers rendezvoused with a score of trucks outfitted with benches and blankets. The marchers quickly boarded the trucks, and with a state police escort, they continued on to Baltimore, where they stayed overnight. The next day, the marchers convened with columns of others in Washington, D.C., to present their protests to Congress, which largely ignored them. The National Hunger March focused attention on the problems of the Great Depression, and the next year, the larger Bonus March convened on Washington, D.C., and stayed for several weeks until President Hoover ordered the army to drive the marchers out of town.

In January 1932, in a letter to the *Delaware Coast News*, Mary C.M. Elliott of the Sussex County Unemployment Relief Committee summarized reports from across the county:

> *Relief work in the several communities of the county seems to be well taken care of, judging from the various reports submitted, but it is apparent as we get deeper into winter months that increased effort on the part of the communities should be made to provide funds for their relief organizations supplemental to the small sum which can be distributed by the County Relief Committee.*

According to Elliott, most of the local committees focused their efforts on providing food and clothing to children in public schools. In addition, Elliott encouraged attendance at the public meetings of the relief committees because it was "most helpful to us in our plans, and we trust the public will continue its interest."[291]

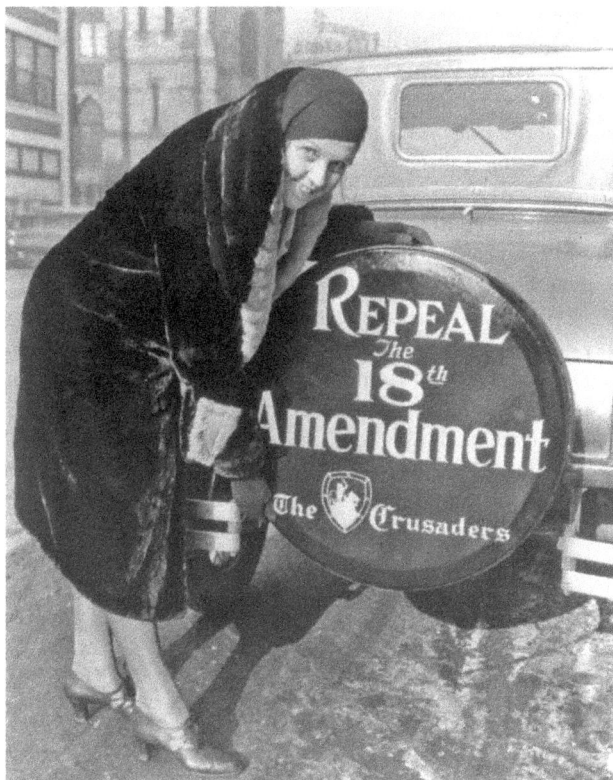

The opponents of Prohibition used all types of methods to promote their cause. *Courtesy of the Library of Congress.*

By November 1932, it had become obvious that the patchwork system of committees and local organizations was insufficient in taking care of the growing number of those in need. Most of the unemployed were concentrated in the Wilmington area, and politicians from the rest of the state objected when it was suggested that the state legislature authorize a $2 million bond issue to help the unemployed. After some wrangling, a $1 million bond issue was passed.[292]

In rural Delaware, where farmers grew much of their own food, people were so short on cash that they resorted to bartering to obtain the goods that they needed. A number of local stores accepted chickens, eggs, milk and other produce items in lieu of cash. Although conditions in some areas of Delaware were not as extreme as they were Wilmington, the number of farm foreclosures continued to rise as the Great Depression maintained its grip on the American economy.

The 1932 presidential election pitted Hoover against the Democratic governor of New York Franklin D. Roosevelt. The Sunday before the election, the *Sunday Morning Star* reported, "Both presidential candidates were racing towards the finish line tonight amid a bedlam of speeches, parades and ear-splitting rallies....Despite the unprecedented driving finish, many already have forecast the election of Governor Roosevelt." The newspaper stated bluntly that "economic troubles overshadow prohibition," and it predicted a sweep for Roosevelt. However, it doubted that the New Yorker would carry Delaware.[293]

The newspaper predicted correctly. Roosevelt won in a landslide, with Hoover carrying only six states, four in New England and Pennsylvania and Delaware, where Sussex and Kent Counties voted for Roosevelt (but the president carried Wilmington and New Castle County). Roosevelt's victory sounded the death knell for Prohibition and took the steam out of any further enforcement efforts. When the new administration took over, the legal limit on beer was raised to 3.5 percent alcohol. Congress passed the Twenty-First Amendment and sent it to the states for ratification; the amendment repealed Prohibition by negating the Eighteenth Amendment. Before Roosevelt's election, Republicans believed that getting the necessary states to ratify the repeal would be difficult, if not impossible.[294] They were wrong.

In January 1933, the state legislature repealed the Klair Law, and the *Sunday Morning Star* editorialized, "The summary disposal of the Klair Law by the legislature...[removes the] hypocrisy, which, for years, have been controlling factors in the legislature's dealings with prohibition, have at last

Four members of the information committee take a break at a meeting of the Women's Organization for National Prohibition Reform. *Courtesy of the Library of Congress.*

loosed their stranglehold on the gullets of our lawmakers or at least of a majority of them."[295]

The newspaper went on to say that many opponents of repeal were sincere citizens who believed that the Klair Law was a powerful and effective weapon against illicit alcohol, but the measure was "one of the most drastic prohibition enforcement laws in the nation…that a law so rigorous must be all the more effective." The opponents included political hypocrites who "knew that prohibition was a myth and prohibition enforcement a farce" but supported Prohibition for political reasons. According to the *Star*, it was a good thing that some of "these double-dealers have been smoked out and now find that their jig is up."[296]

The jig was officially up for Prohibition in Delaware on May 27, 1933, when a statewide referendum was held to determine which parts of Delaware would allow alcoholic beverages to be sold in licensed establishments. All three counties and the city of Wilmington voted overwhelmingly in favor of the licensing system.[297] The *Sunday Morning Star*, which had long believed that Prohibition had been a mistake, editorialized, "We knew if the people of Delaware had a chance to vote, they would be overwhelmingly for repeal. This does not mean that they are any more tolerant of the evils of alcohol. It merely means that they have discovered that prohibition was a tragical farce."[298] Most of the country agreed with Delaware, and the states lined up (the First State was sixth in line) to ratify the Twenty-First Amendment that repealed Prohibition.[299] On December 3, 1933, Utah became the thirty-sixth and deciding state to ratify the Twenty-First Amendment, and Prohibition was officially over.[300] Two weeks later, the *Sunday Morning Star* reported in staccato fashion:

> *Delaware's first formal introduction to* [John] *Barleycorn in fourteen years found reception warmer, drinking still complicated by limited supply of liquor, prices too high for depression consumption. Beer and ale of sterner stuff than farmed 3.2 variety got good hand, five-cent glass hailed. As week ended, reinforcements had come in, stuff plentiful. Bulk buying in stores,*

This dilapidated building in Wilmington once housed a pre-Prohibition bar. *Courtesy of the Library of Congress.*

subject to state supervision. Names taken with each bottle. Drinking prices still very high. First drunk to be arrested was Thomas J. Welsh, picked up at three Wednesday morning. Celebrating gloriously, Thomas very drunk, proud of distinction.[301]

The next week, the *Sunday Morning Star* ran a lighthearted look at the demise of Prohibition that found, "A significant change had come [over] Wilmington's drinking habits. The day of the old saloon, with sawdust on the floor and a family entrance in the rear, was surely in the...past; the days of the speakeasy, when it was smart to be sinful, were no less behind us."[302] Delaware was happy to see John Barleycorn's resurrection.

HAPPY DAYS ARE HERE AGAIN

THE NEW DELAWARE

"Out with the old, in with the new" is a mighty good idea
with which to greet 1933.
—Delaware Coast News

When John Barleycorn returned to Delaware, he found it a changed state. During the more than a dozen years that he had lived underground, many First State residents abandoned the vestiges of the Victorian era and embraced the trappings of the fashion, music and mores of the Roaring 1920s, although, by 1933, many of those changes had been tempered by the Great Depression. But the legalization of alcohol did not mean that Delaware would revert to the corseted dresses and starched collars of the early twentieth century.

In 1920, the passage of the Nineteenth Amendment to the Constitution, which granted women the right to vote, transformed national and state politics. Delaware women were not just advocates for causes, they also voted. Although it took several elections for women to be registered and full participants in the voting process, the change in sentiment regarding the outlawing of liquor may be traced to the number of new female voters who were leaders in the drive to repeal Prohibition.

At the beginning of Prohibition, Delaware had an integrated passenger train and trolley system that enabled residents to visit Wilmington in just a few hours from the most distant towns in the southern part of the state. The Du Pont Boulevard's completion in 1923 made it possible to drive the newer, improved cars with enclosed cabs from one end of the state to the other—from Wilmington to Selbyville on a modern, all-weather concrete highway. Other roads, particularly the Route 13, the corridor south of Dover, were upgraded to be on a par with the Du Pont highway. While bootleggers made extensive use of Delaware's new roads, so did farmers, who were trucking tomatoes, strawberries and other crops to market. Coastal town vacationers also abandoned the train to drive to Lewes, Rehoboth and Bethany Beach.

This change in transportation during the 1920s resulted in a change in drinking habits. In the years before Prohibition, many workers walked or rode a trolley to work. On the way home, they had ample opportunity to stop off at a corner tavern for a tall beer, a shot of whiskey or both. In 1933,

Officers of the Women's Organization for National Prohibition Reform pose at the conclusion of their meeting in 1932. Mrs. Pierre S. Dupont of Delaware, the national vice chairman, is second from the right. *Courtesy of the Library of Congress.*

many more workers walked to their cars, parked near their homes and drove to work. Stopping on the way home to have a drink was less convenient than going straight home. In addition, during the years of Prohibition, Delawareans learned to drink more soda, coffee and water, which flowed freely from more municipal water supplies that were purer and more convenient than the hand pumps in their yards. Although Prohibition was over, vacationers at Rehoboth Beach still drank from the WCTU water fountain that was conveniently located next to the boardwalk.

At the start of Prohibition, home radios were the purview of electronic hobbyists, but when alcohol became legal again, two Wilmington radio stations, WDEL and WILM, broadcast signals that could reach most listeners in Delaware, and no First State home was complete without a radio. Instead of stopping off at a saloon for a strong drink and entertaining conversation, more workers went straight home to relax with their favorite radio program.

The Brick Hotel in Georgetown, before Prohibition, displayed a sign for Stoeckle lager beer (*to the right under the second-floor porch*). *Courtesy of the Delaware Public Archives.*

A more somber Brick Hotel during Prohibition. The sign for Stoeckle beer has been taken down, and a sign indicating that a phone booth was inside was put up. *Courtesy of the Delaware Public Archives.*

The changes in Delaware during Prohibition were echoed in an editorial in the *Delaware Coast News* at the end of 1932, as the end of Prohibition was fast approaching: "We send you the Season's Greetings, with the hope that every day of 1933 will find you a little more happy, more healthy, and more wealthy than the preceding one. We trust there is no reason why 1933 should not be the best years of a lifetime.... 'Out with the old, in with the new' is a mighty good idea with which to greet 1933."[303]

With their principal product outlawed, the three large breweries that had produced Delaware beer in the first two decades of the twentieth century turned to making soda and other legal products, but they did not survive Prohibition. When alcohol became legal again, out-of-state breweries and distilleries dominated Delaware. But as the state laws on alcohol eased, craft breweries began to spring up in the First State. Dogfish Head (named for a cape in Maine) was founded in 1995 by Sam Calagione, and it became the most important brewery in Delaware.[304] In 2019, Dogfish Head Brewery merged with the Boston Beer Company (the makers of Sam Adams Boston Lager) to enable the combined breweries

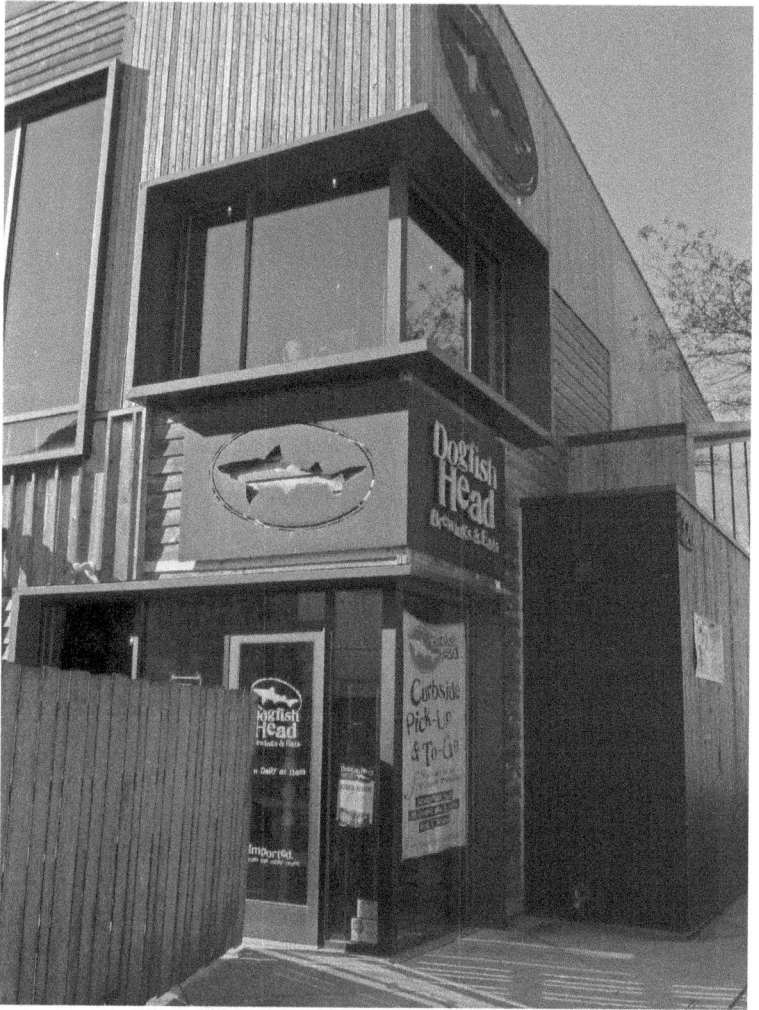

Dogfish Head Brewing and Eats in Rehoboth is an indication of the resurgence of the beer industry in Delaware. *Photograph by Michael Morgan.*

to compete in an industry that was seeing rapid consolidation, as major breweries acquired smaller craft breweries.[305] Although it is tempting to equate the craft brewpubs with the pre-Prohibition saloons that brewed their own beer, the earlier saloons had a seedy reputation that earned the ire of the anti-alcohol forces. On the other hand, Dogfish Head enjoys high standing in the Delaware community and represents the complete rehabilitation of John Barleycorn.

Epilogue

BOOTLEG CHICKENS

During the 1920s, rival gangs continued to use every illegal means, including
murder, to control the marketing and processing of chickens.
—Carol E. Hoffecker, Delaware historian

Prohibition was a time of lawless gun play, colorful characters, warring factions and trucking bootleg liquor across the Delaware countryside. All of these existed before the Volstead Act and the Klair Law, and they continued beyond John Barleycorn's return. A decade before Prohibition, Barnett Baff, a New York chicken dealer, had a flock of enemies, including other dealers, a syndicate that was attempting to corner the poultry market and cohorts of criminals convicted on the basis of Baff's testimony. Baff was attacked by a thug wielding a broken bottle, mysterious fires had been started in some of his stores, his horses had been poisoned and a neighbor who was apparently mistaken for Baff had been murdered.[306]

On November 25, 1914, Baff was at his stall in the West Washington Market, north of Greenwich Village in New York City, when a man approached him with a message that he was wanted outside.[307] Baff generally never ventured from his house or business without being accompanied by a member of his family or a guard. But poultrymen frequently asked for Baff in this manner, so he stepped outside, crossed the street and walked south to Gansevoort Street. Baff was in front of his Brooklyn poultry house on Thirteenth Avenue when two men walked up behind him. One of the men said something, and Baff started to turn around. In true Godfather fashion, one of the men drew a pistol and fired two shots into Baff's back. One bullet hit the poultyman's shoulder, and the other pierced his heart. Baff's assailants quickly jumped into a waiting car and sped off.[308]

After a year-long investigation, during which the police investigated gangs such as the Hudson Dusters and the New York Gophers and interrogated numerous suspects, including Kidd Griffo Cohen, Izzy the Strong Schwitzky, and Big Dave Klondyke, two men, Guiseppi Archiello and Frank Ferrara, were arrested and convicted of Baff's murder.[309]

The Baff murder was just one incident in the New York chicken wars, which were still being fought in the 1920s and 1930s, when Prohibition started and the Delaware chicken industry blossomed. On Delaware's backroads, delivery trucks carrying bootleg liquor were joined by trucks carrying clandestine chicken, and when alcohol became legal again in 1933, bootleggers concentrated on the extralegal chicken business. According to Delaware historian Carol E. Hoffecker:

> *During the 1920s, rival gangs continued to use every illegal means, including murder, to control the marketing and processing of chickens and turkeys in what the newspapers dubbed the "poultry wars" to distinguish them from the look-alike "bootleg wars" that were the scourge of the Prohibition era. Even after the end of Prohibition in 1933 brought respite from the bootleg wars, nothing and no one, not even Mayor Fiorello H. LaGuardia and District Attorney Thomas E. Dewey, proved equal to the poutry men's* price-fixing schemes and gangster tactics.[310]

Vigorous law enforcement efforts eventually drove some of the mobsters from the chicken business, but Sussex County poultry producers had become veterans of marketing bootleg chickens when the United States entered World War II. Driven in large measure by the enormous purchases made by United States Army, poultry prices tripled during the first years of the war. To manage the wartime economy, the Office of Price Administration (OPA) instituted a system of rationing and price controls that fixed the price of poultry, which led to the black market of bootleg chickens.

In April, 1943, the head of the OPA met with Southern Delaware chicken producers at Georgetown High School, and the government officials threatened to take strong action to force the poultry industry to conform to wartime regulations. If the bootlegging continued, they said, the chickens would be seized and turned over to the army. On July 25, 1943, the *Sunday Morning Star* commented, "Before the seizure plan, of what some of the growers term 'legalized hi-jacking' became effective this week, a number

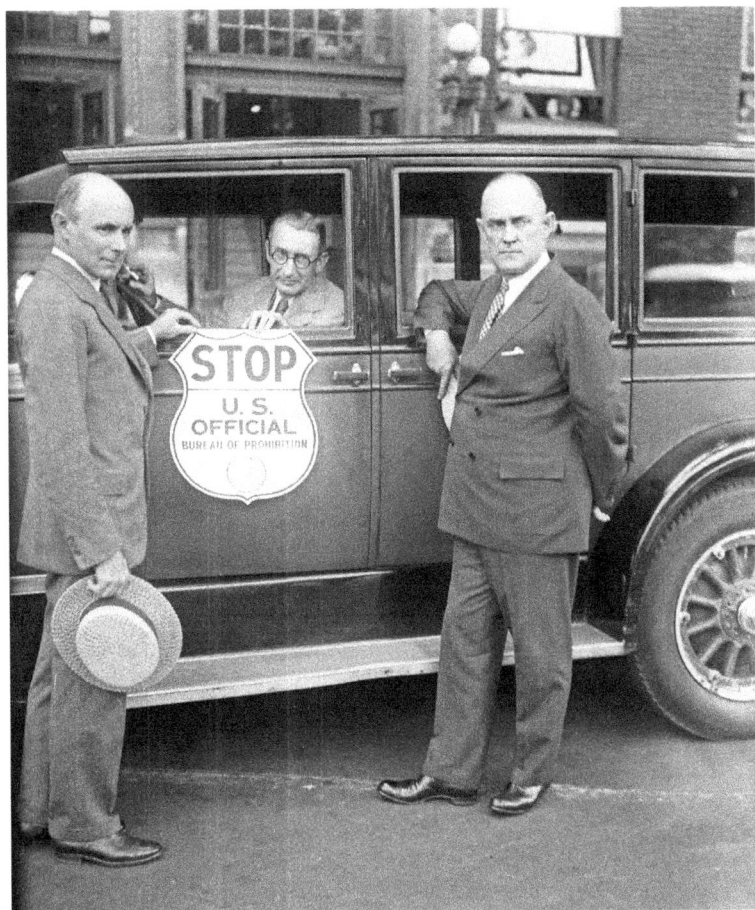

Agents regularly stopped vehicles to inspect them for illegal hooch during Prohibition.
Courtesy of the Library of Congress.

of meetings between OPA representatives and poultry growers were held in an effort to adjust the differences between the ceiling prices and the cost of producing poultry."[311]

The threat of chicken confiscation or "legalized hi-jacking" did not deter the truckers from carrying the bootleg poultry from Southern Delaware. As happened during Prohibition, when checkpoints were set up to look for

During World War II, Delaware State Police stopped vehicles to inspect them for bootleg chickens. *Courtesy of the Delaware Public Archives.*

illegal alcohol, in 1943, roadblocks were set up to check for bootleg chickens. Delaware is roughly shaped like a funnel, with its widest part in Sussex County, the heart of the chicken producing area, and its narrowest section near Wilmington. At Dover, Southern Delaware's two main highways merged, and it seemed logical to set up a chicken checkpoint just north of Dover. The news of the establishment of this roadblock, however, was broadcast over the radio, and the truckers took to the backroads as they made their way north toward Dover. Bystanders, perhaps recalling a similar sight during Prohibition, watched with glee as truck after truck, loaded with chickens, turned off the Du Pont Highway for less-traveled roads until they had made their way around the checkpoint, where it was safe to return to Delaware's premier highway and continue north, unimpeded.[312] As was the case during Prohibition, when many Southern Delaware residents looked the other way when bootleg liquor was trucked to thirsty patrons of speakeasies in the big cities, many Sussex County residents looked with glee on the efforts of the poultry truckers to thwart what many considered legalized hijacking of their chickens. The confiscations of some poultry at the roadblocks and the easing of price ceilings for chickens helped reduce the number of trucks carrying bootleg chickens on Delaware roads. At the end of the war, the growth of chicken processing plants in Southern Delaware helped eliminate the problem altogether.

Bootlegging chickens during World War II was one of the many lessons learned during Prohibition. Delaware residents also discovered that outlawing alcohol did not eliminate drunkenness, crime, poverty or any other social ill. Society's problems demanded a far more complex solution than what was presented a century ago in the "Noble Experiment."

NOTES

Chapter 1

1. Burt, *Poems*, 83–84.
2. "Tonight's the End," *Evening Journal*.
3. Quinn, "Food Ways," 131.
4. Munroe, "Dr. Tilton's Observations," 82.
5. Ibid., 84.
6. Russo, *Delaware Beer*, 17.
7. Ibid.
8. Medkeff, *Brewing*, 7.
9. Quinn, "Food Ways," 131.
10. Shomette, *The Hunt*, 328–34.
11. Hancock, *Two Hundred Years*, 25.
12. *Century of Success*, 29.
13. "Passing of the Saloons Recalls Curious Tales of Old Hostelries," *Sunday Morning Star*, January 4, 1920.
14. Ibid.
15. Medkeff, *Brewing*, 17.
16. Advertisment for Brown's Iron Bitters, *Delaware Pilot*.
17. Avertisment, "Blood Poison," *Evening Journal*.
18. Advertisment, "Stoeckes's," *Sun* (Wilmington).
19. Advertisment, "Hartmann and Fehrenbach Brewing Company," *Sunday Morning Star*.

20. Advertisement, "Duffy's Pure Malt Whiskey," *Evening Journal*.
21. Hancock, "Morgan's Autobiography," 119.
22. Ibid.; *One Hundred Years of Temperance*, 141.
23. Hancock, "Morgan's Autobiography," 119.
24. Ibid., 120.
25. Blakemore, "Activist Carry Nation."
26. Anti-Saloon League Museum, "League Is Formed."
27. C. Wilson, *Pocket Cyclopedia*, 16–17.
28. Bishop-Henchman, "Taxes Enabled Alcohol."
29. "Forth Campaign," *New York Times*.
30. "J. EDWARD ADDICKS," *New York Times*.
31. R. Carter, *Clearing New Ground*, 69–79.
32. *Delaware Pilot*, May 4, 1895.
33. "CONCERNING ADDICKS," *New York Times*.
34. Ibid.
35. Ibid.
36. Human Rights Library, "All Amendments."
37. Methodist Episcopal Church, *Official Minutes*, 51–52.
38. *Bethany Beach Booster* 1, no. 4 (September 1912).
39. Ibid.
40. "JUST A BIT," *Evening Journal*.
41. "Rural New Castle," *Newark Post*.
42. "CITY GOES 'WET'," *Evening Journal*.
43. Ibid.
44. Bartholomew, "War-Scare," 71–74.
45. Human Rights Library, "All Amendments."

Chapter 2

46. Walsh, *Baltimore Prohibition*, 30.
47. *Mill Creek Hundred History Blog*.
48. "INFLUENZA RAMPANT," *Newark Post*.
49. "'FLU' UNDER CONTROL," *Evening Journal*.
50. "PHYSICANS REPORT," *Evening Journal*.
51. Centers for Disease Control and Prevention, "1918 Pandemic."
52. "LIQUOR A REMEDY," *Evening Journal*.
53. Find A Grave, "Briggs."
54. "KEEN ARGUMENT," *Evening Journal*.

55. Ibid.
56. Ibid.
57. Ibid.
58. Ibid.
59. Ibid.
60. Ibid.
61. Ibid.
62. "Happenings," *Middletown Transcript.*
63. "Officially Dead," *Sunday Morning Star.*
64. Ibid.
65. "Taste 'Liquor,'" *Evening Journal.*
66. Ibid.
67. "State and Peninsula," *Middletown Transcript.*
68. "Liquor Seized," *Evening Journal.*
69. "Still Missing," *Sunday Morning Star.*
70. "Rally," *Evening Journal.*
71. Ibid.
72. "K.K. Note," *Evening Journal.*
73. Downey, "'Mercy Master, Mercy,'" 189–91.
74. "Disgusting Sermon," *Evening Journal.*
75. Downey, "'Mercy Master, Mercy,'" 195–98, 200.
76. "K.K. Note," *Evening Journal.*
77. "Bone Dry 1921," *Sunday Morning Star.*
78. "Night Battle," *Evening Journal.*
79. Ibid.
80. Ibid.
81. Ibid.
82. Russo, *Delaware Beer*, 18.
83. Peck, *Prohibition in Washington, D.C.*, 49.
84. Mills, *Chesapeake Rumrunners*, 37.
85. Ibid.
86. "Ring-Leaders," *Sunday Morning Star.*
87. Ibid.
88. Ibid.
89. Walsh, *Baltimore Prohibition*, 11.
90. "Far From Driest," *Evening Journal.*
91. "Navy Planes," *Evening Public Ledger.*
92. Ibid.
93. Ibid.

94. Ibid.
95. "Home Brew," *Evening Journal.*
96. "Far From Driest," *Evening Journal.*
97. Ibid.
98. Ibid.
99. "2,000 'Stills,'" *Evening Journal.*
100. Ibid.
101. "Shots Fired," *Evening Journal.*
102. "Shipload of Rum," *Evening Public Ledger.*
103. "Rum Runners," *Evening Journal.*
104. Ibid.
105. "American Ships," *Evening Journal.*
106. Ibid.
107. "Taxes," *Every Evening.*
108. "Gun Play," *Evening Journal.*
109. Totten, "Reached Its Peak."
110. "Gun Play," *Evening Journal.*
111. "Bootleggers," *Evening Journal.*
112. "Grand Jury," *Every Evening.*
113. "Many Shots," *Every Evening.*
114. Ibid.
115. Ibid.
116. "Dry Agents," *Every Evening.*

Chapter 3

117. "New Opportunity City," *Sunday Morning Star.*
118. Ibid.
119. Ibid.
120. Ibid.
121. Willoughby, *Rum War*, 17.
122. "Clearing State," *Evening Journal.*
123. Ibid.
124. "Prohibition Agents," *Every Evening.*
125. "Too Much," *Every Evening.*
126. "Not So Bad," *Sunday Morning Star.*
127. Willoughby, *Rum War*, 18.
128. "Not So Bad," *Sunday Morning Star.*

129. *Time* (magazine) 4, no. 5 (August 3, 1925).

130. Ibid.

131. "Leaders," *Sunday Morning Star*.

132. "Little Delaware," *Sunday Morning Star*.

133. "World Calls," *New York Times*.

134. "Little Delaware," *Sunday Morning Star*.

135. "World Calls," *New York Times*.

136. Ibid.

137. Ibid.

138. "Little Delaware," *Sunday Morning Star*.

139. Ibid.; Ward, *Continentals*, 499–501.

140. "Little Delaware," *Sunday Morning Star*.

141. "World Calls," *New York Times*.

142. "Little Delaware," *Sunday Morning Star*.

143. "Harding Intiated," *New York Times*.

144. Ibid.

145. "World Calls," *New York Times*.

146. Ibid.

147. "Hooch Victim," *Sunday Morning Star*.

148. Assorted movie advertisments, *Sunday Morning Star*.

149. "Hooch Victim," *Sunday Morning Star*.

150. Ibid.

151. Ibid.

152. Ibid.

153. "Sure Death," *Every Evening*.

154. "Wood Alcohol," *Evening Journal*.

155. Ibid.

156. "Lay Off Booze," *Sunday Morning Star*.

157. Ibid.

158. "'Dragon's Blood,'" *Sunday Morning Star*.

159. Scharf, *History of Delaware*, 1,243.

160. "Story," *State Register*.

161. Laurel Historical Society, "Waller Photographs."

162. "Story," *State Register*.

163. Ibid.

164. "Found Guilty," *State Register*.

165. "Knife Murder," *Philadelphia Inquirer*.

166. Ibid.

167. Ibid.

168. "SENTENCED," *State Register*.

169. *Enforcement of the Prohibition Laws*, 188; "SHOOTING OF ITALIAN," *Sunday Morning Star*.

170. "130 Proff," *Sunday Morning Star*.

171. "WHITEWASH BRUSH," *Sunday Morning Star*; "MR. LAWLESS," *Evening Journal*.

172. "PAULMAN'S ARREST," *Sunday Morning Star*.

173. Ibid.

174. "WHITEWASH BRUSH," *Sunday Morning Star*.

175. "PAULMAN'S ARREST," *Sunday Morning Star*.

176. Ibid.

177. Ibid.; "BLACK SHOT," *Sunday Morning Star*.

178. Totten, "Bootleggers Protected?"

Chapter 4

179. Willoughby, *Rum War*, 45.

180. Ibid., 46.

181. Ibid., 45

182. Ibid., 46.

183. Dring, e-mail, August 13, 2020.

184. Smith, "Historic Vinyard Shipyard."

185. Dring, e-mail, August 13, 2020; Smith, "Historic Vinyard Shipyard."

186. Willoughby, *Rum War*, 47.

187. Ibid., 51–52.

188. Ibid., 62.

189. Ibid., 65.

190. "TO MAKE DRIVE," *State Register*.

191. "POUR LAST," *Sunday Morning Star*.

192. "ELUDE NAVY," *State Register*.

193. Totten, "Moonshiner."

194. "Dapper Dan," *Norwich* (NY) *Sun*.

195. Pauly, "Gatsby," 225–36.

196. "CONVICTED," *Indianapolis Times*.

197. Totten, "Moonshiner."

198. Ibid.

199. Ibid.

200. Ibid.

201. Ibid.

202. "Dapper Dan," *Norwich* (NY) *Sun.*
203. "Outfits Confiscated," *Sunday Morning Star.*
204. "William J. Swain," *Sunday Morning Star.*
205. "Old Gum Boats," *Sunday Morning Star.*
206. "Birds Feeding," *Sunday Morning Star.*
207. "Old Gum Boats," *Sunday Morning Star.*
208. Totten, "Reached Its Peak."
209. E. Carter, "Diary," January 3, 1925.
210. Totten, "Reached Its Peak."
211. Ibid.
212. Ibid.
213. Kotowski, *Ablaze*, 15, 25, 46–48, 53.
214. Totten, "Henlopen Falling."
215. "Light Crashes," *Milford Chronicle.*
216. "Thieves Drive Off," *Evening Journal.*
217. "Rival Bootleggers," *Sunday Morning Star.*
218. Ibid.
219. "Hi-Jackers Prey," *Sunday Morning Star.*
220. Ibid.
221. Ibid.
222. "$50,000 Worth," *Delaware Coast News.*
223. Ibid.
224. Ibid.
225. "Oil and Gas," *Delaware Coast News.*
226. "A Few Words," *Breakwater Light.*
227. Advertisment, Thor Washing Machine, *Evening Journal.*
228. "Home Revolutionized," *Sunday Morning Star.*
229. Memento Mutter, "Violet Ray Generator."
230. "Women Bootleggers," *Sunday Morning Star.*
231. Totten, "Shooting and Being."
232. Ibid.
233. Ibid.
234. Ibid.
235. "'Yes, Dear,'" *Sunday Morning Star.*
236. "Raided Saloon," *Sunday Morning Star.*
237. "Woman Carries," *Sunday Morning Star.*

Chapter 5

238. "PROHIBITON VOTE," *Sunday Morning Star*.
239. Ibid.
240. "DUB DELAWARE," *Sunday Morning Star*.
241. Ibid.
242. Ibid.
243. "'ROMANISM AND RUM,'" *Sunday Morning Star*.
244. "REPUBLICANS," *Delaware Coast News*.
245. Ibid.
246. "NO HOME," *Sunday Morning Star*.
247. "Helpful Tips," *Sunday Morning Star*.
248. Advertisment, Atwater Kent Radio, *Delaware Coast News*.
249. "Debunking," *Delaware Coast News*.
250. "HOLIDAY BOOZE," *Sunday Morning Star*.
251. Ibid.
252. Ibid.
253. "CAFETERIA LUNCHEON," *Delaware Coast News*.
254. "Land of Holly!" *Common Ground*, 1.
255. Sprows, "Delmarva"; Carter, *Clearing New Ground*, 442–44.
256. "PICKED OFF LEWES," *Delaware Coast News*.
257. Ibid.
258. Ibid.
259. Ibid.
260. Ibid.
261. Ibid.
262. H. Wilson, *Dry Laws*, i, 9.
263. Ibid., 16–17.
264. Ibid., 120.
265. Alcohol Problems and Solutions, "Harold D. Wilson,"; H. Wilson, *Dry Laws*, 4.
266. H. Wilson, *Dry Laws*, 14–15.
267. Ibid., 16–17.
268. Ibid., 28–29.
269. Ibid., 29.
270. Ibid., 30.
271. Ibid., 60; "Wilson's Advice," *Sunday Morning Star*.
272. Ibid.
273. "ACCUSE 'THREE GUN,'" *Sunday Morning Star*.

274. Ibid.

275. "ARRESTS NINE," *Sunday Morning Star*.

276. "BOOZE JOINTS," *Sunday Morning Star*.

277. "PLACES RAIDED," *Sunday Morning Star*.

278. "Wilson Speaks," *Delaware Coast News*.

279. Totten, "Bribery."

280. Mills, *Chesapeake Rumrunners*, 141.

281. Ibid., 156.

282. Ibid., 156–57.

283. Meehan, *Day at the Beach*, 164.

284. "Acquit Seven," *Delaware Coast News*.

285. Ibid.

286. Alcohol Problems and Solutions, "Association Against the Prohibition Amendment."

287. Alcohol Problems and Solutions, "Women's Organization for National Prohibition Reform."

288. "HUNGER MARCHERS," *Sunday Morning Star*.

289. Ibid.

290. Ibid.

291. "RELIEF COMMITTEE," *Delaware Coast News*.

292. "Buck Agrees," *Delaware Coast News*.

293. "ROOSEVELT SWEEP," *Sunday Morning Star*.

294. Ibid.

295. "Futile Gesture!" *Sunday Morning Star*.

296. Ibid.

297. "SWEEP DELAWARE," *Sunday Morning Star*; "Wets Win," *Delaware Coast News*.

298. "Fight for Repeal," *Sunday Morning Star*.

299. Delaware Beer History, "Post Repeal."

300. Peck, *Prohibition in Washington, D.C.*, 144.

301. "Barleycorn," *Sunday Morning Star*.

302. "Drinking Habits," *Sunday Morning Star*.

Chapter 6

303. "IT'S 1933," *Delaware Coast News*.

304. Russo, *Delaware Beer*, 56.

305. NPR, "Merger Deal."

Epilogue

306. "MURDER VICTIM," *Star Independent*.

307. "MURDER RICH," *Rock Island Argus*.

308. "CHICKEN DEALERS," *El Paso Herald*.

309. "POLICE NET," *New York Tribune*; "TELEGRAPH TICKS," *Middletown Transcript*.

310. Hoffecker, *John Williams*, 48.

311. "Poultry Men," *Sunday Morning Star*.

312. Ibid.

BIBLIOGRAPHY

Alcohol Problems and Solutions. "Association Against the Prohibition Amendment." www.alcoholproblemsandsolutions.org.

———. "Harold D. Wilson: Harold 'Three Gun' Wilson, Prohibition Agent." www.alcoholproblemsandsolutions.org.

———. "Women's Organization for National Prohibition Reform." www. alcoholproblemsandsolutions.org.

Anti-Saloon League Museum. "Anti-Saloon League Is Formed." www. westervillelibrary.org.

Bartholomew, Robert E. "War-Scare Hysteria in the Delaware Region in 1916." *Delaware History* 27, no. 1, (Spring–Summer 1998): 71–76.

Bishop-Henchman, Joseph. "How Taxes Enabled Alcohol Prohibition and Also Led to Its Repeal." October 5, 2011. Tax Foundation. www. taxfoundation.org.

Blakemore, Erin. "Activist Carry Nation Used a Hatchet to Smash Booze Bottles Before Prohibition." History Stories. History. www.history.com.

Burt, Mary E., ed. *Poems That Every Child Should Know.* New York: Doubleday, Page and Company, 1907.

Carter, Elizabeth "Lizzie." "Diary." Lewes Historical Society Archives.

Carter, Richard B. *Clearing New Ground: The Life of John G. Townsend Jr.* Wilmington: Delaware Heritage Press, 2001.

Centers for Disease Control and Prevention. "1918 Pandemic (H1N1 Virus)." www.cdc.gov.

A Century of Success: The History of the E. I du Pont de Nemours Company. New York: Banker and Investor Magazine Publishing Company, 1912.

Delaware Beer History. "Post Repeal." www.delawarebeerhistory.com.

Downey, Dennis B. "'Mercy Master, Mercy': Racial Politics and the Lynching of George White." *Delaware History* 30, no. 3 (Spring–Summer 2003): 189–210.

Dring, Tim. U.S. Life-Saving Service Heritage Association, e-mail. August 13, 2020.

Enforcement of the Prohibition Laws, Official Records of the National Commission on Law Observance and Enforcement. Vol 1. Washington, D.C.: Government Printing Office, 1931.

Find A Grave. "Dr. Henry W. Briggs." www.findagrave.com.

Hancock, Harold B. *Delaware Two Hundred Years Ago: 1780–1800*. Wilmington, DE: Middle Atlantic Press, 1987.

———. "William Morgan's Autobiography and Diary: Life in Sussex County, 1780–1857." *Delaware History* 19, no. 2 (Fall–Winter 1980): 106–26.

Hoffecker, Carol E. *Honest John Williams, U.S. Senator from Delaware*. Newark: University of Delaware Press, 2000.

Human Rights Library. "All Amendments to the United States Constitution." University of Minnesota. www.hrlibrary.umn.edu.

Jones, Dorothy A. "Charles Gerald Jones—The Man and His Deeds." Typewritten manuscript. Milton Historical Society.

Kotowski, Bob. *Ablaze in Lewes Harbor: The Last Cruise of the SS Lenape*. Wilmington, DE: Cedar Tree Books, 2007.

"Land of Holly!" *Common Ground* (Milton Historical Society Newsletter), Winter 2007.

Laurel Historical Society. "Waller Photographs." www.laureldehistoricalsociety.org.

Medkeff, John, Jr. *Brewing in Delaware*. Charleston, SC: Arcadia Publishing, 2015.

Meehan, James D. *When Life Was a Day at the Beach*. Bethany Beach, DE: Harold E. Dukes Jr., 2007.

Memento Mutter. "Violet Ray Generator, A Stimulating Experience." www.memento.muttermuseum.org.

Methodist Episcopal Church. *Delaware Conference Official Minutes of the Delaware Conference of the Methodist Church*. Federalsburg, MD: J.W. Stowell, March 1908.

Mill Creek Hundred History Blog. www.mchhistory.blogspot.com.

Mills, Eric. *Chesapeake Rumrunners of the Roaring Twenties*. Centreville, MD: Tidewater Publishers, 2000.

Munroe, John A. "Dr. Tilton's Observations on the Propriety of a Farmer Living on the Produce of His Own Land." *Delaware History* 8, no. 1 (Spring–Summer 1998): 77–85.

———. *History of Delaware*. Newark: University of Delaware Press, 1979.

NPR. "Makers of Sam Adams and Dogfish Head Beer Announce Merger Deal." www.npr.org.

One Hundred Years of Temperance. New York: National Temperance Society and Publication House, 1886.

Pauly, Thomas H. "Gatsby as Gangster." *Studies in American Fiction* 21, no. 2 (Autumn 1993): 225–36. www.crmintler.com.

Peck, Garrett. *Prohibition in Washington, D.C.: How Dry We Weren't*. Charleston, SC: The History Press, 2011.

Quinn, Judith. "Food Ways." In *After Ratification, Material Life in Delaware, 1789—1820*. Edited by J. Ritchie Garrison, Bernard L. Herman, and Barbara McLean Ward. Newark: Museum Studies Program University of Delaware, 1988.

Russo, Tony. *Delaware Beer: The Story of Brewing in the First State*. Charleston, SC: The History Press, 2016.

Scharf, J. Thomas. *History of Delaware, 1609–1888*. Vol. 1. Philadelphia: L.J. Richards & Co., 1888.

Shomette, Donald. *The Hunt for HMS De Braak, Legend and Legacy*. Durham, NC: Carolina Academic Press, 1993.

Smith, Jerry. "Historic Vinyard Shipyard Could One Day Be a Part of Milford's Riverwalk." *News Journal*, December 21, 2018. www.delawareonline.com.

Sprows, Amada. "Delmarva and Its Poultry Industry." www.faculty.salisbury.edu.

Walsh, Michael. *Baltimore Prohibition: Wet & Dry in the Free State*. Charleston, SC: The History Press, 2017.

Ward, Christopher. *The Delaware Continentals*. Wilmington: Historical Society of Delaware, 1941.

Willoughby, Malcom F. *Rum War at Sea*. Washington, D.C.: United States Printing Office, 1964.

Wilson, Clarence True, ed. *The Pocket Cyclopedia of Temperance*. Topeka, KS: Temperance Society of the M.E. Church, 1916.

Wilson, Harold D. *Dry Law Facts Not Fiction Comparative Facts, Sensational Dry Raid Facts, Delaware Fact Finder Facts, 1890–1931*. Newark, DE: Press of Kells, 1931.

———. *Dry Laws and Wet Politicians*. Boston: Internal Publishers, 1922.

Newspapers

Bethany Beach Booster 1, no. 4 (September 1912).

Breakwater Light. "A Few Words About Washing." November 15, 1873.

Delaware Coast News. "Acquit Seven in Seizure At Fenwick Island." January 27, 1933.

———. "$50,000 Worth of Liquor Captured by U.S. Coast Guards." November 20, 1931.

———. "Gov. Buck Agrees to a Million Dollar Bond Issue for Relief." November 18, 1932.

———. "Harold D. Wilson Speaks in Lewes." February 27, 1931.

———. "It's 1933—A New Year, a New Era!" December 30, 1932.

———. "Oil and Gas…Causes a Fire"; "Meeting of Sussex County Unemployment Relief Committee." January 5, 1932.

———. "One Hundred and Fifty Bags of Rum Picked Off Lewes Saturday." November 28, 1930.

———. "Republicans Sweep Nation…"; advertisment, Atwater Kent Radio; "Debunking Politics." November 10, 1928.

———. "WCTU of Reohoboth Cafeteria Luncheon." April 20, 1929.

———. "Wets Win in Local Option Election." June 9, 1933.

Delaware Pilot, May 4, 1895.

———. Advertisement for Brown's Iron Bitters. June 15, 1895.

El Paso Herald. "125 Chicken Dealers Accused in Famous Baff Murder Mystery." February 26–27, 1916.

Evening Journal. Advertisement, "Blood Poison." February 1, 1904.

———. Advertisement, "Duffy's Pure Malt Whiskey." November 19, 1909.

———. Advertisement, Thor Washing Machine. November 15, 1917.

———. "Bootleggers in Sussex Worried." March 28, 1922.

———. "Boyce Saves Drink After Night Battle." May 12, 1921.

———. "City Goes 'Wet' By 2,259…" November 7, 1917.

———. "Clearing State of Bootleggers." September 18, 1922.

———. "Delaware Far from Driest." January 12, 1922.

———. "Disgusting Sermon." June 22, 1903.

———. "Estimate 2,000 'Stills' in City." March 27, 1922.

———. "Gets K.K. Note, Thinks It Joke." September 24, 1921.

———. "Getting 'Flu' Under Control at Newark." September 25, 1918.

———. "Gun Play in This Rum Raid." January 19, 1922.

———. "Just a Bit of Liquor for "Dry" Districts." January 23, 1917.

———. "Keen Argument over 'Dry' Bill." April 17, 1920.

————. "Ku Klux Rally…" September 23, 1921.

————. "Liquor a Remedy for Every Ol' Thing!" July 12, 1920.

————. "Making Home Brew in Sussex." August 26, 1921.

————. "Mr. Lawless Soon in His New Hotel." November 3, 1911.

————. "1,000 Gallons of Liquor Seized." July 6, 1920.

————. "Rum Runners on the River." August 9, 1922.

————. "Shots Fired as Four Men Are Nabbed"; "American Ships Now Sell Booze…" June 14, 1922.

————. "Taste 'Liguor,' Aquit Fisher." October 8, 1920.

————. "Thieves Drive Off with Illicit Gin." April 11, 1922.

————. "38 Physcians Report 2,442 'Flu' Cases in City." September 30, 1918.

————. "Tonight's the End of the World for J. Barleycorn…" January 16, 1920.

————. "Wood Alcohol." May 5, 1922.

Evening Public Ledger. "Navy Planes Hunt Coast Rum Ships." July 25, 1921.

————. "Shipload of Rum Watched at Lewes." November 30, 1921.

Every Evening. "Bootlegging Is Encouraged Too Much." February 1, 1922.

————. "Dry Agents Warned." May 15, 1922.

————. "Grand Jury Fails to Indict Lynch…" April 6, 1922.

————. "Many Shots Said to Have Been Exchanged." April 29, 1922.

————. "Moonshine Is Sure Death…" January 28, 1922.

————. "Prohibition Agents at Rehoboth Beach." October 28, 1922.

————. "Taxes from Bootleggers." November 26, 1921.

Harrisburg (PA) Star Independent. "Baff Is Finally a Murder Victim." November 25, 1914.

Indianapolis Times. "'Dapper Dan' Convicted by Woman Jury." April 29, 1929.

Middletown Transcript. "Local Happenings." April 24, 1920.

————. "State and Peninsula." May 8, 1920.

————. "Telegraph Ticks." April 29, 1916.

Milford Chronicle. "Henlopen Light Crashes into Sea." April 16, 1926.

Newark Post. "Influenza Rampant Here." September 25, 1915.

————. "Rural New Castle Goes Dry in Special Election." November 7, 1917.

New York Times. "Addicks's Forth Campaign." July 13, 1902.

————. "Concerning Addicks." November 23, 1894.

————. "Distressed World Calls, Says Harding." June 10, 1923.

————. "Harding Intiated as a 'Tall Cedar.'" June 11, 1923.

————. "J. Edward Addicks, of Gas Fame, Dead." August 8, 1919.

New York Tribune. "BIG POLICE NET CLOSES ON TEN IN BAFF MURDER." December 17, 1914.

Norwich (NY) *Sun*. "Dapper Dan Collins…Dies in Attica." June 21, 1950.

Philadelphia Inquirer. "BROTHER IS CHARGED WITH KNIFE MURDER." December 21, 1924.

Rock Island Argus. "MURDER RICH MERCHANT IS DEEP PUZZLE." November 25, 1914.

State Register. "RUMRUNNERS ELUDE NAVY OFF MD COAST." December 18, 1925.

———. "STORY OF RAID…" January 24, 1925.

———. "THEODORE LYNCH FOUND GUILTY…" February 14, 1925.

———. "THEODORE LYNCH IS SENTENCED TO PRISON FOR LIFE." March 14, 1925.

———. "TO MAKE DRIVE ON BOOTLEGGERS." October 2, 1925.

Sun (Wilmington). Advertisment, "Stoeckes's." February 14, 1898.

Sunday Morning Star. "ACCUSE 'THREE GUN' OF SMALL TACTICS." November 2, 1930.

———. Advertisment, "Hartmann and Fehrenbach Brewing Company." June 9, 1907.

———. "ARRESTS NINE MORE BOOTLEGGERS." November 9, 1930.

———. Assorted movie advertisments. February 22, 1925.

———. "Barleycorn Was Welcome." December 10, 1933.

———. "BIRDS FEEDING ON MASH…" April 12, 1925.

———. "BOSELY'S BRIDE, 17, HOOCH VICTIM…" March 1, 1925.

———. "DELMAR AND SEAFORD BOOZE JOINTS FIND 'THREE-GUN' ON TRAIL." February 15, 1931.

———. "DRY AGENTS PLAN FOR BONE DRY 1921." January 2, 1921.

———. "DUB DELAWARE AS HOTBED OF ORGANIZED VOLSTEAD FIGHTERS." April 1, 1928.

———. "Helpful Tips for That New Radio Set." December 26, 1926.

———. "Henlopen Falling into the Sea Revives Memories of Old Light." April 18, 1926.

———. "HI-JACKERS PREY ON STATE RUMRUNNERS." January 9, 1927.

———. "HOLIDAY BOOZE STILL ROOSTING HIGH HERE." December 16, 1928.

———. "HOME REVOLUTIONIZED BY ELECTRIC DEVICES." May 1, 1927.

———. "'HOOCH' STILL MISSING…" July 18, 1920.

———. "HUNGER MARCHERS IN ORDERLY ARRAY…" December 6, 1931.

———. "John Barleycorn Officially Dead." January 18, 1920.

———. "The Last of a Futile Gesture!" February 5, 1933.

———. "Leaders of Both Drys and Wets…" May 31, 1925.

———. "Mr. Three-Gun Wilson's Advice." October 12, 1930.

———. "No Home Complete Without Radio." November 7, 1926.

———. "Oh, I'm Not So Bad…" December 16, 1923.

———. "Old Gum Boats Used to Store Stockley Bootlegger's Corn." April 26, 1925.

———. "Paulman's Arrest…" November 22, 1925.

———. "Poultry Men of State Silent on Hi-jacking." July 25, 1943.

———. "Pour Last Concrete on Du Pont Boulevard…" November 18, 1923.

———. "President Sees Little Delaware…" June 10, 1923.

———. "Prohibition Post for William J. Swain." April 5, 1925.

———. "Raided Saloon Crowd Cowed by Sleuths." August 30, 1925.

———. "Rival Bootlegers Wage Open Warfare." December 20, 1925.

———. "'Romanism and Rum' Theme…" September 30, 1928.

———. "Roosevelt Sweep Predicted." November 6, 1932.

———. "Shooting of Italian by Federal Sleuths…" April 19, 1925.

———. "Sold 'Dragon's Blood'…" December 14, 1924.

———. "State Prohibiton Vote Shows 87% Against Dry Law." June 17, 1928.

———. "Supt. Black Shot Twice by Cop." October 18, 1925.

———. "Sussex County-Cities Lay Off Booze…" March 26, 1922.

———. "Sweep Delaware for Repeal"; "The Long Fight for Repeal." May 28, 1933.

———. "Three Ring-Leaders in 'Sussex Mule' Sales…" August 6, 1922.

———. "3 Sussex Moonshine Outfits Confiscated." November 30, 1924.

———. "Tonight's the End of the World for J. Barley Corn"; "Nation Dry Tomorrow." January 4, 1920.

———. "Two Lewes Places Raided By Wilson." February 22, 1931.

———. "Water Glass Full of 130 Proff Moonshine…" February 28, 1926.

———. "Whitewash Brush Apllied to Two Cops…" July 12, 1925.

———. "Wilmington…Is New Opportunity City." May 27, 1923.

———. "Wilmington's Drinking Habits." December 17, 1933.

———. "Woman Carries Hugging Cop…" September 26, 1926.

———. "Women Bootleggers Bring Jail Problem." March 21, 1926.

———. "'Yes, Dear,' She Says…" August 23, 1925.

Totten, Edwin C. "Are Bootleggres Protected By Police in Wilmington?" *Sunday Morning Star*, March 7, 1926.

———. "Bribery of Enforcement Agents Not So Common as Believed." *Sunday Morning Star*, February 21, 1926.

———. "Enforcement Reached Its Peak…" *Sunday Morning Star*, February 7, 1926.

———. "Henlopen Falling into the Sea…"; "Shooting and Being Shot at…" *Sunday Morning Star*, February 14, 1926.

———. "Moonshiner Who Boasted That No Man Could Take Him." *Sunday Morning Star*, January 24, 1926.

INDEX

INDEX

ABOUT THE AUTHOR

The author at the Rehoboth WCTU fountain. *Photograph by Madelyn Morgan.*

Michael Morgan, a member of the Delaware Maritime Hall of Fame, has been writing freelance newspaper articles on the history of coastal Delaware for over three decades. He is the author of the "Delaware Diary," which appears weekly in the *Delaware Coast Press*, the *Wave* and the *Salisbury Daily Times*. Morgan has also published articles in *Delaware Beach Life*, *America's Civil War*, the *Baltimore Sun*, *Chesapeake Bay Magazine*, *Civil War Times*, *Maryland Magazine*, *World War II Magazine* and other national publications. His "Lore of Delmarva" weekly radio commentary on historical topics related to the Maryland and Delaware is broadcast by station WGMD 92.7. Morgan's look at history is marked by a lively, storytelling style that has made his writing and lectures popular. Michael Morgan is also the author of *Pirates and Patriots: Tales of the Delaware Coast*; *Rehoboth Beach: A History of Surf and Sand*; *Bethany Beach: A Brief History*; *Ocean City: Going Down the Ocean*; *Civil War Delaware*; *Hidden History of Lewes*; *Delmarva's Patty Cannon*; *The Devil on the Nanticoke*; *World War II and the Delaware Coast*; and *Storms that Shaped the Delmarva Coast*.